PARLIAMENTS IN THE MODERN WORLD

PARLIAMENTS IN THE MODERN WORLD

PHILIP LAUNDY
Inter-Parliamentary Union

Dartmouth

Published by
Dartmouth Publishing Company Limited
Gower House
Croft Road
Aldershot
Hants GU11 3HR

Gower Publishing Company
Old Post Road
Brookfield
Vermont 05036
USA

British Library Cataloguing in Publication Data

Laundy, Philip 1924 –
  Parliaments in the modern world.
  1. Parliaments
  I. Title
  328'.4

ISBN 1-85521-042-8
ISBN 1-85521-055-X pbk

Contents

vi

Foreword

There are now 145 national Parliaments throughout the world. This unprecedented number not only reveals how much almost all peoples of this planet have achieved in setting up sovereign states but also shows that legislative assemblies have become very widely recognised as irreplaceable instruments expressing the popular will for the governance of the nation.

Indeed, the institution of Parliament has been constantly championed and the process of the emancipation of peoples significantly promoted by the Inter-Parliamentary Union (IPU) throughout its first hundred years of existence. It is therefore only natural that, among the activities to mark its Centenary, the IPU has chosen to publish a book giving a broad picture of Parliaments, showing the rich diversity which stems from their evolution over the years and from their adaptation to different national conditions.

For some time, the IPU has provided scholars and specialists with the worldwide encyclopaedia of legislatures *Parliaments of the World*, the latest edition of which* makes a detailed survey of the structure and working of each of 83 national assemblies.

But the governing bodies of IPU had in mind a different kind of book to mark the Centenary celebration: not a work of reference containing a myriad of data compiled after a wide-ranging and lengthy international inquiry, but rather a view of the world's parliamentary landscape seen through the eagle eyes of an observer who, from his vantage point, could focus on the outstanding features of the panorama spread out before him.

The IPU found this keen observer in the person of Mr Philip Laundy, Clerk Assistant of the Canadian House of Commons, already well known in academic and parliamentary circles for his earlier publications on Parliaments of the British Commonwealth.

While preparing this book, Mr Laundy tapped the resources of the IPU's International Centre for Parliamentary Documentation and those of the Canadian Library of Parliament, and has enriched those

---

*Edited by Dartmouth Publishing Company Limited, Aldershot, 1986

findings with his own research; he has admirably carried out the task entrusted to him and has written a book which will certainly arouse the interest of people from all walks of life.

The author could not have succeeded without the understanding and support of the Speaker of the Canadian House of Commons, to whom the IPU wholeheartedly acknowledges its debt of gratitude. That support is further proof of the attachment which Canada has unfailingly shown since joining our organisation at the outset of this century.

When welcoming the participants to the first Conference of the IPU on 29 June 1889, Senator Jules Simon, former Prime Minister of France, reminded them: 'Representing divers nations of the world, we can make the most excellent use of the greatest power which exists – that given us by the electors.'

One hundred years on, parliamentary power is being exercised in ever-widening areas which touch almost all aspects of the lives of most of the inhabitants of the globe. This book explains the parliamentary structures and mechanisms through which that power is channelled, controlled and made effective.

Pierre Cornillon
Secretary General
Inter-Parliamentary Union
Geneva
January 1989

Foreword

THE HONOURABLE JOHN FRASER, M.P.
SPEAKER OF THE HOUSE OF COMMONS
CANADA

The publication of this book marks a highly significant parliamentary occasion, the centennial of the Inter-Parliamentary Union. It is a particularly important contribution to the literature of Parliament since it deals with the subject on a global basis. Numerous books have been written on the legislative and representative institutions of specific countries, but comparative studies embracing a wide range of the Parliaments of the world are far more rare; in fact, I know of no other work of this nature which provides such an extensive coverage. It is designed for a general readership, and while not over-burdened with detail it is nevertheless richly informative. I believe that teachers, students and parliamentarians themselves will derive great value from it.

Of particular satisfaction to me is the major contribution made by the Canadian House of Commons to the realization of this project. When Philip Laundy, the Clerk Assistant, was approached by the Inter-Parliamentary Union and requested to undertake this challenging work, I had no hesitation in authorising his release from his normal duties so that he could accept. Canada has always been a staunch supporter of the Inter-Parliamentary Union and its outstanding work in promoting co-operation and understanding among the parliamentarians of the world. It has demonstrated that national frontiers and differing systems of government need not be barriers to constructive communication between the world's legislators. Its centenary in 1989 calls for special recognition and this book will be an enduring feature of a landmark year. We are honoured that a Canadian has been selected to prepare it, and, if I may say so, the Union will have no reason to regret its choice. We are also delighted to have contributed other services, including the preparation of the indexes of the English and French editions by the Index Branch of the House of Commons, and the secretarial and other support required by the author in the course of his work. The Canadian House of Commons is proud to have been so closely involved in the centenary preparations.

I hope this book will command the wide readership it deserves. I commend it to parliamentarians of all nations and to those they represent, being confident that parliamentary institutions will continue to flourish for the continued betterment of mankind.

John A. Fraser
House of Commons
Ottawa 1989

Preface

Writing this book has been a richly rewarding experience, and I am grateful to have been given the opportunity. For this I must thank the Inter-Parliamentary Union for inviting me to prepare their centennial project and the Canadian House of Commons for releasing me from my normal duties, thus enabling me to accept the invitation.

In embarking upon this project my enthusiasm was tempered with apprehension as I realised I was facing a formidable challenge. While I have a long experience in the service of Parliament, and have been exposed to the operation of many of the Parliaments of the world, there were many others about which I knew very little. I therefore had a great deal to learn, and this book could not have been completed without the extensive co-operation and facilities which were so generously accorded to me from various sources.

I must first of all acknowledge the contribution of the IPU's Consultative Committee of Experts, chaired by Mr. V. Purushotha-man, member of Lok Sabha, India, who monitored the project from its inception. They provided me with my guide-lines, explained their requirements and commented constructively and critically on the first draft which was submitted to them. For two extended periods I worked at the IPU headquarters in Geneva where I had access to their files and much unpublished material. During these periods I received very full and cordial co-operation from Mr. Pierre Cornillon, Secretary-General of the IPU, and his colleagues. I was made to feel completely at home, as 'one of them', and was touched by the many courtesies and kindnesses I received from all the members of a very special international team with whom it was a pleasure to work. These two visits enabled me to pursue much of the essential research and locate information which would not have been easily obtainable otherwise.

During a visit to London I was given access to the files and unpublished documentation of the Commonwealth Parliamentary Association headquarters, for which I have to thank the Secretary-General, Dr. David Tonkin. The CPA, unlike the IPU, does not have a global membership, but its activities embrace a large number of the Parliaments of the world nevertheless. Having been actively associated with the CPA for some 30 years, and an honorary member for 20,

I was not exactly a stranger to Dr. Tonkin and his colleagues. I was given the usual warm welcome for which I would like to record my appreciation.

Indispensable to me in the preparation of this book was the wide range of contacts I was able to make with officers from Parliaments around the world. They are known by various designations – Clerks, Secretaries-General, Librarians – and all of them are experts in the operations and procedures of their differing assemblies and systems of government. Many of them, particularly those from Commonwealth Parliaments, have been my friends for many years. In the course of my learning experience I have made many new friends, thanks largely to the opportunity of attending the meetings of the Association of Secretaries-General of Parliaments, held simultaneously with conferences of the IPU. My debt to them all is very great. Thanks to them the horizons of my parliamentary knowledge have broadened considerably. I hope that the benefits of this enlightenment will shine forth in this book, although if they do not the fault will be mine alone.

A limiting factor in my research has been the fact that I am competent to work in two languages only, namely English and French. Fortunately for me, many countries whose national languages are other than English or French publish official material and explanatory literature in the two languages which I understand. A great deal of such material is available at IPU headquarters, but I must also express my gratitude to the staff of various Embassies here in Ottawa who have supplied me with valuable documentation in translation. I would acknowledge in particular the co-operation I have received from officers of the Embassies of Austria, Brazil, China, Italy, the Soviet Union and Switzerland, because of the personal nature of these contacts and the lengths to which they have gone to provide me with up-to-date information and material. Brazil has recently adopted a new constitution, and as I write radical constitutional reforms are taking place in the Soviet Union. I am grateful to my friends in the diplomatic service of their countries for keeping me abreast of current developments.

One of the problems involved in preparing a book of this kind is that of balance. This book is designed for a popular readership, and I have therefore tried to avoid excessive detail. At the same time, if a book is to have any value at all it must not be over-simplified. It is my hope that parliamentarians, those who serve them, academics and the students whom they teach, will find this book as informative as those who read it simply for the sake of interest. The fact remains that a great deal more information is available concerning some Parliaments than others, and it has been necessary to be selective in deciding where to place the emphases. The treatment given to the various assemblies of the world is admittedly unequal, but it is hoped that those which have received closer attention will serve as comparative illustrations of the different systems they represent.

A book with any pretensions to scholarship will normally be well documented. In the case of this book, for reasons explained below, footnotes have been kept to a minimum and used only where it is necessary to acknowledge a direct quotation or for purposes of elaboration. Most of the documentary sources consulted have been constitutions, rules or standing orders of the various assemblies, proceedings of parliamentary conferences and professional associations and unpublished material. In addition I have been impressed by the amount of useful information contained in brochures handed out to visitors by many Parliaments, information which has the advantage of being up-to-date. I have also engaged in direct correspondence with colleagues in many parts of the world. As far as books are concerned, my principal source of reference has been the major two-volume work of reference entitled 'Parliaments of the World', the second edition of which was published for the Inter-Parliamentary Union in 1986 by the Gower Publishing Group. Some of the content of this impressive compendium is unavoidably out-of-date but it remains a rich repository of parliamentary information. Given the nature of my sources, and the fact that the literature relating to Parliaments is vast in the case of some countries and non-existent in the case of others, I have decided to keep footnotes to a minimum rather than underline disparities. For the same reason I have decided not to include a bibliography.

A special acknowledgment is due to the Honourable John Fraser, Speaker of the Canadian House of Commons, and Mr. Robert Marleau, the Clerk of the House, for their unstinting support of this project, without which I would have been unable to embark upon it. I acknowledge also the support and encouragement of Mr. Charles Lussier, recently retired as Clerk of the Senate of Canada, who remains at the time of writing the President of the Association of Secretaries-General of Parliaments and a member of the Consultative Committee of Experts which initiated and monitored the project. I have had the benefit of close contact with him throughout its preparation. Finally I acknowledge the indispensable contribution of my secretary, Mrs. Pierrette Pretty, who produced the several drafts of the text and incorporated the many revisions required in the course of writing the book. Her skill in the use of a word processor was a boon to us both.

Philip Laundy
Ottawa, 1989

1   The Diversity of Parliaments

What is a Parliament?

Parliaments exist in most of the countries of the world, although the word is not universally used to describe a representative assembly. The term 'Parliament' is usually associated with the British system of parliamentary government, a system which has influenced the development of representative assemblies in many parts of the world. In pre-revolutionary France the word *'Parlement'* was applied to courts of justice which were not representative bodies at all. The word itself is derived from the Latin *'parliamentum'* and the French word *'parler'* and originally meant a talk; and talking is, of course, what Parliaments do most of the time. The origins of Parliaments and similar assemblies can be traced back hundreds of years. They are the central institutions of many systems of government. Although conceived in ancient times, they seem to be infinitely adaptable and their numbers have proliferated and developed many forms in modern times. Even in countries which have experienced *coups d'état* they frequently re-emerge. It is interesting to note that when the Inter-Parliamentary Union was founded in 1889 nine countries were represented. By 1989 the number had risen to 112. In the world as a whole, 145 countries have Parliaments of one kind or another at the time of writing.

    In the context of this book the term 'Parliament' embraces many widely differing assemblies: the United States Congress, the Congress of People's Deputies and the Supreme Soviet of the USSR, the Japanese Diet, the National People's Congress of China, the *Knesset* of Israel, to name just a few. It is important to bear in mind that some Parliaments consist of two chambers, in which case they are called bicameral, while others consist of only one, and are therefore unicameral. In some countries the head of state is a constituent part of Parliament. When one speaks of the British Parliament, for example, the term encompasses the Queen, the House of Lords and the House of Commons, the three constituent parts which together form the

1

whole. The Queen, represented by a Governor-General, is also a constituent part of the Parliaments of those countries of the Commonwealth in which she remains head of state, countries which include Australia, Canada, New Zealand and a number of the smaller member-nations. Her role has become a largely formal one, involving the opening, prorogation and dissolution of Parliament and assenting to bills which have been adopted by the respective chambers, functions which are normally performed on the advice of the governments concerned.[1] It is also the function of the Queen and her Governors-General to ensure the stability of the system of government. This responsibility is normally discharged by appointing as Prime Minister the leader of the party commanding a majority in the elected House. The choice of a government is a matter for the electorate.

The United States Congress consists of the Senate and the House of Representatives, the Supreme Soviet of the USSR of the Soviet of the Union and the Soviet of Nationalities, the Japanese Diet of the House of Representatives and the House of Councillors. Other bicameral Parliaments include those of Argentina, Australia, Brazil, Canada, France, India, Italy, Mexico, Philippines, Thailand and West Germany. However, bicameral Parliaments are not only to be found in the populous nations of the world. The Bahamas, Barbados, Jamaica, Trinidad and Tobago, and even some of the very small Commonwealth countries of the Caribbean have Parliaments consisting of an appointed Senate and an elected lower House. At the other end of the scale, the National People's Congress of China, which has the world's largest population, is a unicameral body. In the Soviet Union the Congress of People's Deputies, provided for under the revised constitution, elects the Supreme Soviet from among its own members. Most of the countries of Africa with functioning Parliaments have opted for unicameral assemblies, an exception at the time of writing being Zimbabwe. By contrast, most of the Congresses to be found in the countries of Latin America are bicameral, their structure having been influenced to some extent by the United States model. Three of the socialist states of Eastern Europe have bicameral assemblies: Czechoslovakia, which is a federal state consisting of two nations, Yugoslavia and Poland, where a bicameral system was recently introduced. A bicameral system is also under consideration in Hungary. Western European countries with unicameral Parliaments include Denmark, Finland, Greece, Luxembourg, Portugal and Sweden. Denmark and Sweden abolished their second chambers in 1954 and 1971 respectively. Other countries to have done likewise are New Zealand, where the second chamber was abolished in 1950, and Sri Lanka where it was abolished in 1971. Most Western

2

European countries have bicameral Parliaments, although the Parliaments of Norway (called the *Storting*) and of Iceland (called the *Althing*) divide themselves into two chambers following each general election. In Norway one quarter of the members form the upper House and three-quarters the lower House. In Iceland the proportions are one third and two-thirds respectively. In the Middle East and Mediterranean region, unicameral Parliaments are in the majority, these being the choice of Cyprus, Israel, Malta and the Arab states with the exception of Jordan. South Africa is probably unique in having a Parliament of three chambers, one consisting of white members, one of Asians and one of Coloureds (persons of mixed race). Black South Africans, who comprise the majority of the population, are not enfranchised, and the reality of power resides with the white chamber.

Parliaments also vary greatly in size. China's National People's Congress numbers 2,978 members, while at the other end of the scale the tiny Pacific nation of Tuvalu has a legislature of only twelve. Each chamber of the Supreme Soviet of the USSR had 750 members before the revision of the constitution. The Caribbean nation of Antigua and Barbuda also has a bicameral Parliament in which the two Houses are numerically equal – the Senate and the House of Representatives each has seventeen members. One could go on making similar comparisons, but perhaps the point has been made. The size of a Parliament is obviously influenced by the size of the population, and in federal countries, where the people enjoy representation at more than one level of government, the size of the central Parliament is likely to be smaller than in the case of a unitary state with a similar population.

Upper Houses and Lower Houses

The chambers of a bicameral Parliament are usually referred to as the upper House and the lower House. The term 'second chamber' normally refers to the upper House but there are exceptions to every rule. In the Netherlands the upper House is the First Chamber and the lower House is the Second Chamber. In most countries with bicameral Parliaments the lower House is usually the popularly elected and more powerful of the two Houses, but again one dare not generalise. Some upper Houses are also popularly elected, some have equal powers with the lower House and some have even greater powers. The United States Senate is the prime example of a powerful upper House. Like the House of Representatives it is directly elected and it has powers, such as the ratification of treaties and the confirmation of high-ranking federal appointments, which are not enjoyed by the lower House. By contrast Japan's House of Councillors, although popularly elected, is subordinate to the House of Representatives. The latter controls the budget, approves treaties with foreign powers and is recognised as the pre-eminent chamber.

The prime example of an upper House with very limited powers, yet bolstered by the prestige attaching to an ancient institution, is the British House of Lords. While it remains in principle an hereditary body, it has been reinforced over the past three decades by the creation of life peers and the admission of women. Originally the more powerful of the two Houses, the powers of the House of Lords were drastically curtailed by the Parliament Acts of 1911 and 1949. The earlier Act resulted from a constitutional crisis provoked by the House of Lords in rejecting the budget of the then Liberal government in 1909. Today the House of Lords is a greatly transformed body, its power to obstruct legislation being limited in nearly all instances to one of delay, yet it is by no means without influence. Although it numbers about 1,200 members, its active membership is a minority of the total and of this the life peers form a very substantial proportion.

Upper Houses come in many varieties and no one may be said to be typical. Lower Houses, on the other hand, usually have the common element that in one way or another they are elected. Another common denominator is their primacy in matters of finance. In nearly all bicameral Parliaments the initiative in financial matters belongs to the lower House. The argument over the bicameral versus the unicameral system is of long standing and will probably always persist. It has been said that if the second chamber disagrees with the other it is mischievous, if it agrees it is superfluous. On the other hand the advocates of the bicameral system, notable among whom was John Stuart Mill, have argued that if too much power is vested in a single assembly it may tend to become arrogant and overweening. Upper Houses are composed by various methods. Some are entirely elected, some entirely appointed, some partially elected and partially appointed. Sometimes indirect forms of election are employed, methods of appointment can also vary, and an upper House often provides the means of representing special interests either through appointment or election. An upper House is often seen as performing a 'watchdog' function, particularly where constitutional matters or human rights are concerned. The argument that a second chamber provides the opportunity for sober second thoughts is probably less persuasive than it once was. It certainly carries no influence with those who advocate the abolition of the House of Lords or the wholly appointed Canadian Senate since such people are opposed to non-elected assemblies on principle.

Bicameral Parliaments in Federal Countries

Perhaps the most telling justification of a bicameral system can be made in relation to countries with a federal system of government. In an assembly based on representation by population the populous states or provinces will inevitably swamp the smaller ones. The balance can be redressed in an upper House where the states or provinces are given equal representation. It was on this basis that the United States Congress was established. In the House of Representatives 150 of the 435 members are returned by five large states: California, New York, Texas, Pennsylvania and Ohio. Six of the smallest states return only one Congressman apiece. However, each of the fifty states, regardless of its size, returns two senators, so that in the upper House tiny Vermont is represented on equal terms with mighty California. Because of the system of government, the powers of the legislature being separated from those of the executive, the United States Senate is able to perform effectively as the protector of states' rights. Australia is also a federal nation with a popularly elected Senate in which each of the six states is equally represented. However, it is a part of a different system of government, the British parliamentary system, whereby the executive is responsible to the legislature and cabinet ministers are members of one House or the other. Australian parliamentarians are bound by party discipline to an extent which does not occur in the United States, and it is doubtful that the Australian Senate plays such an active role as the United States Senate as a protector of the states.

There are three other federations in the Commonwealth: Canada, India and Malaysia, each with a bicameral Parliament, the upper House being constituted quite differently in each case. The Canadian Senate has 104 members and is wholly appointed. Originally appointments were for life but since 1965 a retirement age of 75 has been in force. The ten Canadian provinces are not equally represented in the Senate, but when the Canadian federation was created in 1867 from the four original provinces (Quebec, Ontario, Nova Scotia and New Brunswick) the Senate was composed on the basis of regional equality. The subsequent adherence of other provinces and the granting of representation to the two territories in the North upset the regional balance and today the Senate cannot claim to be a House of the provinces in a truly realistic sense. For all practical purposes appointments to the Senate are in the gift of the Prime Minister of the day and most of them are made on a party basis. Constitutionally the powers of the Senate are equal to those of the lower House, the House of Commons, except that it cannot initiate financial legislation. Nowadays it generally accepts a more passive role in the parliamentary process, recognising that it would be inconsistent with modern concepts of parliamentary democracy were it to exert its powers to the full.[2] There is widespread support in Canada for Senate reform, even among senators themselves, but agreement has yet to be reached on a plan of reform.

The Indian Parliament consists of the House of the People (*Lok Sabha*) and the Council of States (*Rajya Sabha*), the latter being the upper House which consists of not more than 250 members, twelve being nominated by the President, the rest elected by electoral colleges consisting of the elected members of the legislative assemblies of the states and union territories. The method of election is proportional representation by means of the single transferable vote. The nominated members are selected from among people who have distinguished themselves in such fields as the arts, sciences and social services. The states are represented in proportion to their size. The Council of States has special powers in relation to constitutional issues, but it has no controlling power and was never intended to be the equal of the House of the People. The Vice-President of the Republic is the President of the Council of States, a practice borrowed from the United States where the Vice-President presides over the Senate. This was probably seen as a means of adding prestige to a body with limited powers. India is not a typical federation since the central government is very strong, being even empowered to suspend the constitutions of the states.

Malaysia's Parliament consists of a House of Representatives (*Dewan Rakyat*) and a Senate (*Dewan Negara*), the latter consisting of 68 members. Malaysia's thirteen states are each represented by two members elected by the state legislative assemblies and two members are appointed to represent the federal capital of Kuala Lumpur. However these 28 representatives form only a minority of the total membership, the remaining 40 being appointed in recognition of their distinguished service in various fields of endeavour or as representatives of racial minorities. In most circumstances the Senate's power is one of delay only, and the power of appointment provides the government with a means of controlling a majority of the seats.

In the United States a senator's term of office is six years, one third of the membership retiring every two years. Elections for one third of the Senate take place every two years coincidentally with elections for the entire House of Representatives. Australian senators are also elected for a six-year term, one half retiring every three years, although in certain circumstances a double dissolution of both Houses can take place. India's Council of States is not subject to dissolution but one third of its members retire every two years. The term of a senator in Malaysia is three years and no one person can serve for more than six years, either continuously or otherwise. A

6

senator's term of office is not interrupted by a dissolution of Parliament, which affects only the lower House.

In the Federal German Republic, the Federal Council (*Bundesrat*), the upper House, consists of 45 members, 41 of whom represent the states (*Länder*). The remaining four are appointed with limited voting rights by the Senate of West Berlin. It exemplifies the logical concept of a federal upper House. The eleven states are represented in proportion to their populations, each having a minimum of three votes. Not only are its members appointed by the governments of each of the eleven states, but they are themselves members of their own state governments. By this means the state governments participate directly in the federal parliamentary process. Appointments to the *Bundesrat* are made or renewed by each state government following a state election. Switzerland is another federal country with a bicameral Parliament consisting of the National Council (*Nationalrat*) and the Council of States (*Ständerat*), both having equal powers. Each of the 20 cantons sends two members to the *Ständerat* and each of the six half-cantons sends one for a total of 46, the method of their election and the length of tenure being decided entirely by each canton. The cantons thus have exclusive control over the composition of the Council of States, once again exemplifying the logical principle of a second chamber in a federal system of government. Austria's federal Parliament consists of a popularly elected National Council (*Nationalrat*) and an upper House (*Bundesrat*) consisting at the present time of 63 members elected on a proportional basis by the nine provincial assemblies. Representation of the provinces in the *Bundesrat* is determined by population, the minimum number of members being three and the maximum twelve.

The world's largest federation both in terms of population and geographic extent is the Soviet Union and its Supreme Soviet consists of two chambers, the Soviet of the Union and the Soviet of Nationalities. Each has equal powers, so that the use of the terms 'upper' and 'lower' House would be inappropriate. At the time of writing the Soviet Union is passing through a period of constitutional transition and the status of the Supreme Soviet will be affected. Previously it was the highest body of state authority, each chamber consisting of 750 members. Under the new constitution the highest body of state authority is a Congress of People's Deputies, consisting of 2,250 deputies composed as follows: 750 from territorial electoral districts with equal numbers of voters; 750 from ethnic territorial electoral districts; and 750 from national public organisations. This Congress elects from among its own number a new Supreme Soviet which will be accountable to the former. The new Supreme Soviet will be the permanent legislative, administrative and control body of state authority, and will continue to consist of two chambers, each having 271 members. One of its functions will be the convening of the sessions of the Congress of People's Deputies. The Soviet Union is a nation of many nationalities and the new electoral system will continue to reflect this ethnic and cultural diversity. The 750 deputies of the Congress of People's Deputies representing the ethnic territorial electoral districts will be composed as follows: 32 representing each of the 15 union republics; eleven representing each of the twenty autonomous republics; five representing each of the eight autonomous regions; and one representing each of the ten autonomous areas. These proportions are the same as those which composed the Soviet of Nationalities of the former Supreme Soviet.

Yugoslavia's federal constitution makes provision for an assembly system at the apex of which is the Assembly of the Socialist Federal Republic of Yugoslavia consisting of two chambers. The Federal Chamber consists of 30 members from each of the six republics and 20 from each of the two provinces. The Chamber of Republics and Provinces consists of members from each Republican and Provincial Assembly. Each Republican Assembly returns twelve members and each Provincial Assembly eight. Thus, both Houses reflect the federal nature of the country, by means of equality of representation between states and between provinces, and through the direct representation in the Chamber of Republics and Provinces of deputies from these levels of government.

Argentina, Brazil and Mexico are examples of Latin American countries with a federal system of government. Civilian government was restored in Argentina in 1983 and the constitution previously in force before the imposition of military rule was re-adopted. In the case of Brazil, civilian government was restored in 1985 and elections for a National Congress to act as a constituent assembly took place in 1986. A new constitution was adopted in 1988. All three Latin American federations share certain features in common with the United States, notably the separation of powers. All three have bicameral Congresses comprising in each case a Senate and a Chamber of Deputies. The latter, as in the case of the United States House of Representatives, is elected on the basis of representation by population. In Mexico the Senate consists of 64 members, two from each of the 31 states and the federal district directly elected for a six-year term, half of them retiring every three years. In Argentina the Senate consists of 46 members, two nominated by each provincial legislature and two from the federal district. A senator's term of office is nine years, but one third of the membership must retire every three years, the order of retirement being determined by the drawing of lots. In Brazil each of the 23 states and the federal district are represented by 3 senators for a total of 72. Under the constitution adopted in 1988 they are all directly elected by the people and serve an eight-year term. They retire on a rotational basis and are eligible for re-election. In Mexico an exclusive power of the Chamber of Deputies is the consideration and approval of the budget and an exclusive function of the Senate is the analysis of the President's foreign policy.

Bicameral Parliaments in Other Countries

Although France is not a federal state, the French Senate is designed to ensure the representation of the territorial units of the republic and the representation of French citizens living abroad. It consists of 319 senators indirectly elected for a nine-year term by an electoral college in each department or overseas dependency, one third of them retiring every three years. The electoral colleges are formed of the members of each departmental council (or its equivalent in overseas territories) and each municipal council within the respective departments. Metropolitan France is represented by 296 senators, the overseas departments and dependencies by 13, and 10 seats are reserved for French citizens living abroad. Although the Senate has significant powers it could in the final analysis be overruled by the National Assembly acting alone under provisions detailed in the constitution. Italy's Senate of 315 members is also representative of the regions and is directly elected for five years. Each region has at least seven senators and the President of the Republic may nominate up to five from persons who have distinguished themselves in the arts, sciences and social service. The Senate of Spain, another upper House most of whose members are directly elected, includes among its 208 directly elected members, four representing each of the 47 mainland provinces, regardless of population. Additional members are elected by the Parliaments of the autonomous communities.

Territorial representation is only one of the functions which an upper House can perform. For example, the Irish Senate (*Seanad Eireann*), which consists of 60 members, is designed to represent a wide spectrum of interests. Apart from 11 who are appointed by the Prime Minister, the others are indirectly elected with a view to recognising the claims of all the social, professional, commercial and cultural interests of the country. Six senators are elected by the two universities and 43 by an electoral college consisting of the members of the lower House (*Dail Eireann*), the local authorities and sitting senators.

There is perhaps another reason why many unitary states also have bicameral Parliaments. In some countries the legislative load is so heavy that an upper House can co-operate by relieving the pressure on the lower House. It can deal with less controversial issues, including complex legislation which is not politically divisive, and it can devote time to matters which the lower House cannot fit into its own programme. Since being shorn of its powers, the British House of Lords has rendered valuable service in such areas, and also as a House of review. Amendments proposed by the Lords to bills sent up from the Commons are frequently accepted by the lower House.

In smaller countries which have bicameral Parliaments, the upper House may have yet another purpose to serve. The Commonwealth countries of the Caribbean which have bicameral Parliaments have already been referred to. In each case the upper House is composed in a similar manner, the majority of the members being appointed on the advice of the Prime Minister, a smaller number on the advice of the Leader of the Opposition. In Jamaica, for example, the proportions are 13 and 8 for a total of 21. A recent election which the opposition declined to contest left the government holding all the seats in the House of Representatives, thereby leaving a vacuum in the Senate as there was no Leader of the Opposition to advise on the eight opposition appointments.[3] In normal circumstances, however, the provisions relating to the Senate would enable a weak opposition to strengthen its representation through its power of appointment to the upper House. At the first general election to take place in Grenada following the restoration of parliamentary government, one opposition member was returned. As Leader of the Opposition he was entitled to nominate three members to the Senate. In Barbados and Trinidad and Tobago, where the numbers of senators nominated by the Prime Minister and Leader of the Opposition are twelve and two and sixteen and six respectively, the constitutions provide for an additional number of senators to be appointed by the head of state at his own discretion. The President of Trinidad and Tobago appoints nine and the Governor-General of Barbados seven. In the Bahamas, where the Prime Minister controls nine Senate appointments and the Leader of the Opposition four, the Governor-General appoints three more after consultation with both. The upper House in these countries therefore serves to improve the equilibrium in the balance of representation.

Provincial and State Legislatures

Parliaments also exist in the component states or provinces of federal countries, and in some cases they are bicameral. All fifty of the United States of America have bicameral legislatures save one, Nebraska, which abolished its upper House in 1937. In Australia five of the six states have bicameral Parliaments, Queensland being the exception, and the Northern Territory has a unicameral legislative assembly. Canada's ten provinces all have unicameral legislatures, although some of them were once bicameral. Quebec was the last province to abolish its upper House in 1968. In Canada the term 'legislature' is used to distinguish the provincial assemblies from the central Parliament. The centrally administered territories of Yukon and the North-West Territories also have unicameral legislatures. Of India's 24 states, five have bicameral legislatures and the rest are unicameral. All of Malaysia's state legislatures are unicameral. In the Soviet Union, Soviets exist at every level of government and every constituent republic has its own Congress of People's Deputies and Supreme Soviet, the latter being elected by the former under the revised constitution.

The Representative Function of Parliament

Parliaments perform a variety of functions which may be defined as legislative, financial, deliberative, critical, informative and representative. Perhaps the true common denominator, regardless of a country's political system, is that of representation. Nearly every parliamentary assembly – perhaps it may not be too risky to say all such assemblies – have a representative function. Even the modern British House of Lords, which can hardly be said to be representative under any contemporary definition of that term, was once effectively representative of the nobility and the church, and developed from the advisory councils of the mediaeval Kings of England. Even today it might claim to be representative of certain interests through the appointment of life peers and the inclusion of the two archbishops and 24 bishops who continue to represent the Church of England. It also serves the function, probably unique among Parliaments, of being the highest court of appeal in the United Kingdom. The Canadian Senate, a wholly appointed body, is often derided as being non-representative, yet without a Senate designed to represent the regions of the new federal nation, Canada would never have come into existence as a united country. It has been said of the House of Lords that it provides positive proof of life after death, and of the Canadian Senate that its members represent only themselves and they enjoy the unbounded confidence of their constituents. These are good jokes, worth a chuckle, but they overlook the useful work that these bodies, unrepresentative though they may be, regularly perform.

Although some Parliaments provide for the representation of special interests, the essential function of a popular assembly is the representation of the people as a whole. Political systems differ, with

11

the result that some Parliaments have a multi-party membership, some consist of two parties ranged against each other and some reflect the exclusive dominance of a single party. Countries with an electoral system based on proportional representation are likely to have several, or even a multiplicity of, parties represented in their Parliaments. The two-party Parliament is more likely to emerge where the simple plurality system is in operation, the United States being the outstanding example of a country where the competition for power is virtually restricted to two parties. One-party Parliaments are mostly to be found in countries where only one party may legally exist.

The Difficulty of Making Comparisons

This introductory chapter should serve to indicate the wide diversity which exists among the Parliaments of the world. The reader who has read thus far will undoubtedly realize that it is not always easy to make comparisons – in fact in many cases to attempt to do so would be dangerous and misleading. It is impossible, for example, to compare in any realistic manner the United States Congress with the Supreme Soviet of the Soviet Union. Both serve their purpose within the structure of their respective societies. The principle of the one-party state is completely incompatible with the systems operating in the Western democracies. Yet numerous countries have turned to the one-party system in order to overcome disunity and achieve political stability. It does not always guarantee success, as numerous *coups d'état* throughout the world have demonstrated, but *coups* have also taken place in countries operating multi-party systems. It has perhaps been too readily assumed by former colonial powers that their own parliamentary systems are suitable for export in any circumstances. It is remarkable that so many third world countries have succeeded in adapting alien systems to their own requirements and establishing their own form of parliamentary government. Although this book will attempt to do more than present bare facts, its aim is not to judge whether any one system is better than another, but rather to emphasise their diversity, at the same time pointing out their similarities.

Notes

1   In Australia, however, in 1975 the Governor-General took the extraordinary step of dismissing the federal government. Such an occasion indicates that circumstances can still arise in which a constitutional head of state can have a decisive role to play.

2 Although in 1987 and 1988 it fought very strongly to secure amendments to certain controversial bills.
3 The seats were filled on the advice of the Prime Minister by persons who were not members of the governing party after the main opposition party declined to propose names. A subsequent election held in 1989 was contested by both main parties and restored normality to the representative system.

2   Electoral Systems

Qualifications of Voters and Candidates

Like Parliaments themselves, electoral systems vary greatly. While there are few common denominators, the majority of countries with parliamentary assemblies have universal adult suffrage, the minimum voting age in most cases being 18. In Austria it is 19, in Japan, South Korea, Switzerland and the tiny Pacific republic of Nauru it is 20, and in a number of other countries, most of which are in Africa, it is 21. In Cuba and Nicaragua the voting age is as low as 16, and similarly in Yugoslavia if the youthful voter is employed. The voting age has also been reduced to 16 in Brazil under the new constitution adopted in 1988. In order to vote in Indonesia one is required to be 17 or married, and 17 is also the voting age in North Korea. In Western Samoa the voting age is 21 but the vote is limited to *matais*, the elected heads of families, who may be male or female. The enfranchisement of women is virtually universal today. New Zealand, where female suffrage for national elections was first introduced in 1893, can claim to be the first country to have implemented this reform. In Jordan women voted for the first time in 1984, and in Switzerland women obtained the right to vote in federal elections in 1971 following a referendum. In Egypt women are registered as voters by their own request but not automatically. Few countries impose a literacy qualification on voters, although in Brazil this requirement was abolished as recently as 1985. In the United States federal law prohibits the kind of voter registration tests which were once required by the electoral laws of some states and which operated in a discriminatory manner. The small Pacific country of Tonga requires its voters to be literate. In South Africa the right to elect members to the House of Assembly, the principal legislative chamber, is restricted to white citizens. Under a recently adopted constitution, Asians and Coloureds (persons of mixed race) may elect members of their own race to separate chambers. Black South Africans, who form the majority of the population, remain disenfranchised and play no part in the parliamentary electoral process. In some countries, notably Argentina, Australia, Belgium, Cyprus, Italy, North Korea and Turkey, voting is compulsory. In Brazil it is compulsory between the ages of 18 and 65. In Paraguay it is compulsory unless one is over 60, and in Peru unless one is over 70. In Switzerland it is compulsory in some cantons. In Egypt voting is compulsory for men. In New Zealand and Senegal registration, but not voting, is compulsory.

In many countries, anyone who is qualified to vote may stand for election, but there are some significant exceptions. In the United States a candidate for the House of Representatives must be at least 25 and a candidate for the Senate at least 30. The same age requirements in respect of the lower and upper Houses are to be found in Argentina, India, Japan, Pakistan and Uruguay. In Peru a deputy must be at least 25 and a senator at least 35. In France the age requirements are 23 for the National Assembly and 35 for the Senate. In Belgium and Italy the minimum ages for election to the Chamber of Deputies and the Senate are 25 and 40 respectively. In Italy, although the voting age for the lower House is 18, one must be 25 to be eligible to vote for the Senate. In the Netherlands 25 is the minimum age for election to either chamber. The minimum age for election to the unicameral assemblies of Egypt and Turkey is 30, to those of Algeria, Gabon and Tunisia 28, and to those of Cyprus, Ecuador, Greece, Malawi, Mali, Monaco, Morocco, the Philippines and Zaire, 25. Twenty-one is the minimum age for candidates in a number of countries, and in Cameroon, Côte d'Ivoire and Romania, it is 23. Some countries impose a literacy requirement upon candidates for election, and these include Botswana, Cameroon, Costa Rica, The Gambia, Kenya, Malawi, the Philippines, Sierra Leone, Singapore and Zambia. In most countries elections are conducted by secret ballot. Many countries require deposits from candidates in order to discourage frivolous candidatures. The deposit is normally returned to every candidate polling a specified minimum percentage of votes.

The 'First-past-the-post' System and its Variations

In this chapter we shall proceed to describe the electoral systems which operate in various countries. An electoral system is bound to be influenced by the political nature of the state. It would be idle to pretend that electoral abuses never occur or that intimidation and corruption are never involved in the electoral process. Our purpose, however, is to describe the systems and not to investigate abuses. The simplest system of all is one that has frequently been criticised as producing the least representative result. This is the plurality or, as it is sometimes called, the 'first-past-the-post' system, whereby the candidate securing a larger number of votes than any of his or her opponents wins the seat. This system operates in the United States,

Great Britain and most of the countries of the Commonwealth. It normally operates on the basis of single-member constituencies, and if every constituency in a general election were contested by only two candidates it might still produce an unbalanced result. For example, it is possible for one party to win every seat with a simple majority, leaving the minority totally unrepresented. Alternatively, if a majority of the seats were won by one party with narrow majorities and a minority won by the other party with overwhelming majorities, the party winning the election might well do so with a minority of the popular vote. Where constituencies are contested by more than two candidates, the potential for imbalance is even greater. In a constituency in which three candidates each poll an almost equal number of votes, the winning candidate having a slight edge, it could be won by as little as 34% of the vote. With more than three candidates it could be won by an even smaller percentage. Under this system the result depends on the distribution of votes and it is quite common for a party to win an election with a lower percentage of the popular vote than its nearest rival, or to win an overwhelming majority with only a minority of the popular vote. The British general election of 1987 provides an illustration of what can happen. Out of a total number of 650 seats, the Conservatives won 374 with about 42% of the popular vote. The Labour Party won 227 with about 27% of the popular vote, and with a substantial 25% the Liberal-SDP Alliance only managed to win 22 seats. The Conservatives won a comfortable majority of 102 seats over all other parties with the support of only a minority of the voters. The only hope for a third party under this system would lie in a concentration of support in certain regions rather than an even distribution of support across the country.

It is because of the uneven results produced by this system that in those countries where it operates there are many advocates of proportional representation. Needless to say the parties which suffer from the system are among the advocates, but the major parties which benefit from it usually seek no change, arguing that for all its faults it makes for stable government. Proportional representation is far more complex and exists in many forms, but before considering the systems of those countries where it operates, there are variations of the 'first-past-the-post' system which should be dealt with first. In Australia elections to the House of Representatives are determined by the preferential or alternative vote. The system in use for the Senate is the method of proportional representation known as the single transferable vote, which we shall be considering later. The preferential vote is relatively simple in its operation and is designed to prevent a candidate winning a seat with a straightforward plurality. The voter is invited to number the candidates on the ballot paper in the order of his or her preference. If no candidate polls an overall majority of votes, the candidate with the least number of votes is eliminated and those votes are redistributed according to the preferences expressed, the process continuing until one candidate emerges with an overall majority. The system does not guarantee a proportionately balanced result, and it can be criticised for giving a second or third preference the same weight as a first preference in the redistribution process. It does, however, allow the voter to give his or her first preference to a third party without the risk of 'wasting' the vote completely.

France has probably changed its electoral system more frequently than any other country. It has twice been changed since 1985, when a system of proportional representation was introduced. After one general election had been held under this system, the electoral law was amended on 9 April 1986 to revert to the former two-ballot majority system, which is a variation of the 'first-past-the-post' system. The only candidates declared elected on the first ballot are those who obtain a clear majority over the combined votes of their opponents. This usually occurs only in a small minority of constituencies. At one time, under this system, there was no limit to the number of candidates who could participate in the second ballot, even candidates who had not participated in the first ballot being eligible. Since the establishment of the Fifth Republic, a candidate for the National Assembly may take part in the second ballot only if he or she gained as a minimum a specific percentage of the votes of the registered electorate in the first ballot. The second ballot is decisive and the leading candidate wins the seat whether or not an overall majority is gained, as in the 'first-past-the-post' system. The two-ballot system is also used in presidential elections, but only the two top candidates in the first ballot are eligible to compete in the second.

Mixed Systems

One of the criticisms directed against proportional representation is that it reduces the personal contact between a member and his or her constituency. All P.R. systems depend on multi-member constituencies, and under some systems party lists are employed which can reduce still further the direct relationship which members have with their electorates when they represent single constituencies. The electoral system of West Germany incorporates an interesting compromise. One half of the members of the *Bundestag* (excluding the 22 who represent West Berlin) are directly elected in single constituencies. The other half are selected from lists submitted for each state by each political party. The voter has two votes, one being cast for the constituency member, the other for a party list. To win seats a party

17

requires at least 5% of list votes unless at least three of its members have managed to secure constituency seats. The list seats are allocated according to a system devised by Victor d'Hondt. They are allotted according to a quotient reflecting the highest average of votes cast, each party securing a seat for each full quotient of votes cast in its favour, remainders being disregarded. The West German system enables parties which might have difficulty winning constituency seats to secure representation by means of the lists.

Variations of the West German system are to be found in some countries, including Mexico, where a new electoral law came into force in 1987. Three hundred deputies are elected in single constituencies by simple majorities. Two hundred are elected by proportional representation in five multi-member constituencies from regional party lists. No single party is allowed to obtain more than 350 seats all told and access to the proportional representation seats is designed to favour not only the minority parties, but also a party which, having gained 51% of the popular vote in the single-member constituencies, has failed to win an equal or higher proportion of those seats. South Korea operates a system which greatly favours the strongest party. One hundred and eighty-four members of the National Assembly are elected in 92 dual-member constituencies by simple majority. Of the 92 remaining seats, two thirds are allocated to the party winning the largest number of the other seats, the remainder being proportionately distributed among other parties which have captured at least five elective seats. Senegal operates a mixed system whereby 60 members are elected by simple majority and 60 by proportional representation from party lists, no split or preferential voting being allowed. Similar systems operate in Madagascar and Venezuela.

Proportional Representation: List Systems

Some list systems enable voters to vote for individual candidates, while others do not. A number of countries employ closed lists, the choice of the elector being limited to a party list, the party itself deciding which of its members shall occupy seats in the legislature. Israel and Guyana are among the countries which operate closed lists and in both cases the entire country is treated as a single constituency. The 120 seats in the *Knesset* are distributed proportionately in accordance with the d'Hondt system, the threshold being one per cent, which means that a party securing as little as one per cent of the total vote could qualify for a seat. In Guyana's 82–seat National Assembly, the 53 elective seats are allocated by dividing the total number of votes cast by 53, thus determining the quota required in order to win a seat. The systems in Austria, Portugal and Spain

18

require closed lists based on separate constituencies, each province being a constituency. Spain's Parliament, the *Cortes*, is bicameral, both chambers being popularly elected by the same method, except for two deputies in the lower House who are elected by simple majority. In Austria's upper House, the *Bundesrat*, the seats are divided among the parties according to the number of seats they hold in the provincial assemblies. Portugal's Parliament is unicameral and the number of names on each party list must equal the number of seats to be filled in each of the 22 constituencies. Japan's upper House, the House of Councillors, is popularly elected under a system introduced in 1983 which favours the larger parties. To be eligible for election a party is required to present a list of at least ten candidates, at least five of them being existing members of Parliament, or to have polled at least 4% of the popular vote at the previous election. One hundred of the 252 members are elected nationally, the remainder representing local constituencies.

The closed list system is to be found in a number of Latin American countries, although there are variations to be noted. In Brazil it is in use for the Chamber of Deputies, in which the states are represented by a minimum of eight and a maximum of 70 deputies according to the size of their populations. The Senate is popularly elected by the simple majority system. In Argentina senators are also elected by simple majority, but by the provincial assemblies. In Guatemala's unicameral Congress, 25 members are elected on a proportional basis from a national list, and 75 by proportional representation for constituencies each of which returns at least two members. In Uruguay the party list system operates for both Houses, the country forming a single constituency for Senate elections. Closed list systems are also used in Colombia and Peru and for the unicameral Parliaments of Costa Rica and Ecuador. In Paraguay the voting system greatly favours the majority party, two-thirds of the seats in both Houses going to the party winning the most votes.

Some list systems offer the voter much greater flexibility. Nearly all the countries of Western Europe use proportional representation in one form or another and the most flexible systems allow voters to exercise various options. They can simply vote for a party list, split their votes between lists or vote for individual candidates. In the Netherlands, where the entire country forms a single constituency as in Israel, the elector, while voting for a list, may also express a preference for a candidate on that list. The quota is calculated by dividing the total number of votes cast by 150, the size of the membership of the lower House. In Italy a voter may express three preferences in a constituency returning 16 members and four in one returning more than 16. An additional number of national seats are distributed on the basis of the greatest remainder, provided a party has won at least one seat and 300,000 valid votes. For elections to the National Council of Switzerland each of the 26 cantons constitutes a constituency. Five of them return only one member, and in these cases the candidate with a simple majority is elected. In the others a proportional method known as the Hagenbach-Bischoff system is used, and electors can vote for a party list, split their votes, or vote for candidates on different lists. In Belgium all 212 members of the Chamber of Representatives and 106 of the 182 senators are directly elected using party lists. There is no provision for vote-splitting, but preferences for a main and a substitute candidate may be expressed.

It is perhaps in the Scandinavian countries that the most flexible, albeit complex, systems are to be found. Denmark has an electoral system which is designed to reflect the popular vote as accurately as possible. Of the 179 seats which comprise the *Folketing*, 175 represent mainland Denmark. Of these, 135 are elected by constituencies which each return from two to fifteen members. The remaining 40 seats are distributed among the parties on a national basis. The electoral quotient is determined by the St. Laguë system, which favours minor parties by dividing the total number of votes cast by a number larger than the number of seats available, thereby producing a more proportional result than the d'Hondt system. The St. Laguë system is also used in Norway and Sweden. In the former each county constitutes a constituency returning between four and fifteen members to the *Storting*, which comprises 157 members. Candidates may run simultaneously in several constituencies, and if elected in more than one they must select the one they wish to represent. Of the 349 members of the Swedish *Riksdag*, 310 are returned by 28 constituencies. A party requires 4% of the national vote or 12% of a constituency vote to qualify for a seat. Thirty-nine compensatory seats are distributed on the basis of the total votes cast, although parties profiting from the 12% rule are excluded from this process. Finland and Iceland operate somewhat different systems. The 200 members of Finland's *Eduskunta*, except for one who is elected by simple majority vote, are returned by fourteen constituencies on the basis of party lists. Seats are distributed among the parties or alliances of parties in accordance with the d'Hondt method, and candidates are ranked according to the number of personal votes they have polled. Iceland's 63-member *Althing* consists of 40 members representing seven constituencies, 14 representing the city of Reykjavik, and nine national members chosen to balance the party representation according to the percentage of the popular vote received by any party capturing at least one constituency seat. Flexible systems are also to be found in Cyprus, Liechtenstein and Luxembourg. Monaco, which constitutes a single constituency for electoral purposes, allows vote-splitting but not the expression of preferences for individual candidates.

The Single Transferable Vote and Single Non-Transferable Vote

A system of proportional representation which does not make use of party lists is the single transferable vote. Under this system the political parties nominate candidates in multi-member constituencies, enabling the voter to vote for individuals rather than parties. Voters may indicate their choice of candidates by numbering them in order of preference, all candidates who poll the necessary quota of votes being declared elected. For example, in a constituency returning four candidates the quota would be one quarter of the votes cast plus one, because three other candidates could not each have more. Surplus votes go to swell the totals of the other candidates according to the preferences expressed. Candidates who fail to obtain the quota are eliminated and their votes are also distributed according to the preferences expressed, the process continuing until the number of candidates remaining in the poll equals the number of vacancies. The system enables voters to stack their preferences for candidates of the same party or to divide their options, as they choose. It is used in Ireland to elect the 166 members of the *Dail Eireann*, in Malta to elect the 69 members of the House of Representatives, in Australia for Senate elections, in the Australian state of Tasmania, and in India for the election of those members of the Council of States who are chosen by the state assemblies. It is claimed for the system that no vote is wasted because it provides for the distribution of preferences.

In contrast with the single transferable vote is the single non-transferable vote, the system used for elections to the lower House of the Japanese Diet. Apart from one constituency which returns a single member, there are 130 districts which each return between three and five members. The elector votes for only one candidate in each district and the winners are those receiving the largest number of votes. To be elected a candidate's votes must equal at least one quarter of the number produced after dividing the total of the valid votes cast in each district by the number of seats to be filled.

Electoral Systems in Socialist States

Elections in the Soviet Union and other socialist states take place within the framework of a different kind of constitution from those of Western countries. The constitution of the Soviet Union provides for the social and economic foundations of the state. It enshrines the

21

leadership of the Communist Party, which is the only legal party in the state. In terms of the constitution power belongs to the people and is exercised, under the revised constitution, through Congresses of People's Deputies, the socialist ownership of the means of production being the foundation of the economic system. Congresses of People's Deputies exist in all the union republics and at the highest level of the state. The Supreme Soviet of the USSR and the Supreme Soviets of the union republics are elected by the Congresses of People's Deputies. Together with governmental institutions they constitute a single system of bodies of state authority. Every region, area, district, city and village has its own representative body, and a citizen may not normally be a member of more than two Soviets simultaneously. The rights and duties of a deputy are specified in the constitution. Deputies are not professional parliamentarians, and it is expressly provided that they shall not discontinue their regular employment, although the revised constitution provides that members of the Supreme Soviet of the USSR shall be released from their employment or production duties for the whole duration of their term of office. They represent a wide range of occupations and professions, many being workers and peasants, many having considerable experience in government. Unlike some Parliaments which sit throughout the year the plenary sessions of the Soviets have not, in the past, been of long duration, but this is likely to change in the light of the reforms which, at the time of writing, are in the process of implementation.

In November 1988 an amendment to the constitution and a new electoral law were adopted by the Supreme Soviet, which at the time was the highest body of state authority. Under the amended constitution the highest body of state authority will be a Congress of People's Deputies consisting of 2,250 members elected under the provisions of the new electoral law. There will be no limit to the number of candidates who can be nominated and the influence of the Communist Party in the selection of candidates is expected to be reduced. Elections will be conducted by electoral commissions consisting of representatives of work collectives, public organisations, meetings of voters at their places of residence and of servicemen in military units. There will be 750 territorial electoral districts each returning a single member by direct suffrage, all the groups composing the electoral commissions having the right to nominate candidates. Another 750 members will be representatives of public organisations elected at congresses or conferences of these organisations, the ratio of representation being as follows: 100 deputies from the Communist Party; 100 deputies from the trade unions; 100 deputies from co-operative organisations; 75 deputies from the All-Union Leninist Young Communist League; 75 deputies from women's councils united by the Soviet Women's Committee; 75 deputies from organisations of war and labour veterans united by their All-Union Council; 75 deputies from scientists' associations; 75 deputies from artistic unions; and 75 deputies from other public organisations and citizens' associations established by law. The distribution of the 750 ethnic territorial electoral districts will conform to the quotas of which the Soviet of Nationalities of the Supreme Soviet was formerly composed. Nominations for the territorial and ethnic territorial electoral districts must be made at a general meeting within the constituency consisting, in most instances, of at least 500 persons. Candidates once nominated will have the right to campaign for election through the mass media and by addressing public meetings.

As explained previously, the new Supreme Soviet will no longer be directly elected, but elected instead by the Congress of People's Deputies from among their own members. It will continue to consist of two chambers, each consisting of 271 members instead of 750 as before. One fifth of the members of both chambers will be re-elected annually. As the permanent legislative organ of the system of government it is likely to remain in session for longer periods than its predecessor. It is expected to be more directly involved than its predecessor in the oversight of government institutions and the determination of legislative and other national issues.

Under the previous electoral system candidates were selected at public meetings, and although various groups had the right to nominate candidates, the selection process was largely dominated by the Communist Party. Once the selection had been made a single list was presented to the voters who could accept or reject it as it stood. Although not in every way identical, the electoral systems of the socialist states of Eastern Europe bear some resemblance to that of the Soviet Union prior to the adoption of the new electoral law, although at the time of writing, political reforms are in the process of being implemented in Poland and Hungary. In both countries the formation of opposition parties will be permitted. Poland has introduced a bicameral system and in Hungary this is an option which is being considered. All the socialist countries contemplate the possibility that there will be more candidates seeking election than there are seats to be filled, and in Poland and Hungary, there is a requirement, pre-dating the reform process, that at least two candidates must be fielded for each constituency. In these two countries provision is also made for the appointment of national members. Thirty-five of the 460 members of the Polish Sejm are important public figures selected from a national list, and in Hungary 35 of the 387 members of the National Assembly are chosen in like manner. Bulgaria, Czechoslovakia, the German Democratic Republic and Romania, all make provision for a second electoral round in cases where a candidate has not secured an absolute majority of the votes. The single list on which all candidates appear is in each case endorsed by the Communist Party or the national coalition led by the party.

The National People's Congress of China is indirectly elected, as are the congresses at the lower levels of government except at the basic community level (districts, small municipalities, villages) at which elections are direct. China describes itself as a democratic dictatorship of the people, the apparent paradox probably resulting from difficulties of translation. The dictatorship of the proletariat, formed of the alliance between workers and peasants, is held to include all who work for a living, this therefore being the majority of the people whose rights are protected within the framework of the socialist system. Since the system is designed to work for the good of all the people, those who would seek to undermine it are regarded as the enemies of the people and the government will invoke the dictatorial power of the state to suppress them. The representative system is very complex. Constituencies are delimited by means which are not necessarily geographical, the place of work usually being preferred as an electoral base to the place of residence. At this level direct elections take place for local assemblies, the candidates being nominated by the Communist Party, the eight democratic parties regarded as patriotic, popular organisations and groups of electors. It is provided that there should be 50% to 100% more candidates than there are seats to be filled, and candidates require an absolute majority in order to be elected. Rural deputies represent larger communities than those elected for urban constituencies. Representation of national minorities is guaranteed no matter how small their communities may be.

Other levels of representation in ascending order include autonomous districts and larger municipalities; provinces, autonomous regions and the three municipalities of Beijing, Shanghai and Tianjin, which deal directly with the central government; and, at the supreme level, the National People's Congress itself. The deputies at these levels are selected by the assemblies immediately below in such a way as to interpret the will of the electors. The process involves extensive discussion behind closed doors. Electoral procedure at the basic level is supervised by a standing committee of the local assembly, which also determines the number of members of which the assembly is comprised. At the other levels it is supervised by electoral commissions:

In Yugoslavia direct elections take place for communal assemblies which in the past elected the 220 members of the Federal Chamber. However, in the light of constitutional reforms in the process of implementation at the time of writing, elections to the Federal

Chamber and to the assemblies of the republics and provinces will in future be direct. In Cuba the National Assembly of 510 members (which is quite sizeable for a country of 10 million people) is indirectly elected by the members of the 169 municipal assemblies which are directly elected by the people.

Elections in the One-Party States of Africa

In the one-party states of Africa the selection of candidates is controlled by the ruling party, but the electors are usually given a choice, and in most cases the successful candidate needs only a simple majority to win the seat. In most of these countries the nominating process constitutes a primary stage at which the competition can be very keen. For example, at the 1983 election in Cameroon, 2600 candidates, all members of the ruling party, competed for the 120 National Assembly seats. A final list of 120 names, a blocked list, was presented to the electorate, which in this case had no other choice. In the 1988 election, the National Assembly having been increased in size to 180 members, only 324 candidates in 49 constituencies competed for these seats. On this occasion, voters were able, for the first time, to choose between two rival lists. Congo and Gabon also have a primary stage which results in a blocked list being presented to the electorate. In Benin the electoral process involves three stages which result after consultation in a blocked list. In Congo candidates need not necessarily be party members and of the 153 assembly seats 68 are allotted to the ruling party, 55 to mass organisations, 10 to the armed forces and 20 to the country's regions and the capital. Zambia's constitution was amended in 1983 to abolish primary elections and provide for the direct adoption of candidates, who must be members of the ruling party, by the central committee of the party. However, the committee selects more candidates than there are seats to be filled so that electors are offered a choice. Malawi limits the number of candidates to five per constituency. In Algeria it is provided that there shall be three times as many candidates as there are seats to be filled. At the 1983 election in Kenya 750 candidates competed for the 158 elective seats of the National Assembly. For the 1988 election, the number of elective seats having been increased to 188, a system of primary elections was introduced. The system required party members in each constituency to line up behind the candidate of their choice, a candidate requiring a minimum of 30% support in order to be eligible for the general election itself. Electors are given a choice of candidates in Côte d'Ivoire, Mali, Sierra Leone, Tanzania and Togo, while in Djibouti and Somalia they are presented with a blocked list. In Côte d'Ivoire independent candidates are permitted to stand for election. Members in most of these countries represent separate constituencies, Cameroon and Somalia being among the exceptions. In both cases the entire country is regarded as a single constituency for electoral purposes.

Unusual Electoral Systems

The constitution of Fiji, prior to the *coup d'état* of 1987, provided for a unique electoral system which made use of four electoral rolls. The 52 members of the lower House consisted of 22 Fijians, 22 Indians, and eight who were neither Fijian nor Indian. Voters on the National Roll, which consisted of all registered electors on the three communal rolls, elected ten Fijians, ten Indians and five members of other races. The Fijian Communal Roll elected 12 Fijians, the Indian Communal Roll 12 Indians, and the General Communal Roll three members of other races. The system was devised to protect the representation of the native Fijians who are outnumbered by the Indian community. It nevertheless permitted an Indian-led party to win the general election of 1987, a result which provoked a Fijian-led *coup*. The Fijian constitution also made provision for an appointed Senate.

Another unusual electoral system was enshrined in the independence constitution of Zimbabwe, an African country which formerly had a multi-party system. The constitution reserved 20 of the 100 seats in the House of Assembly for white members, a very high proportion in view of the small size of the white community. White voters were entitled to register on either the separate white voters' roll or the common roll. The constitution provided for the abolition of these white seats after seven years provided a two-thirds majority of the House approved, and this was effected in 1987. Twenty of the members of the House of Assembly are now elected by the other 80 sitting as an electoral college. The constitution also provides for a Senate of 40 members, 24 being elected by the House of Assembly, ten representing tribal chiefs and six being appointed by the President.

Representation of Women and Special Interests

In some unicameral Parliaments, provision is made for the inclusion of members who are not directly elected and who often represent special interests. In Morocco 102 of the 306 members of the legislature are indirectly elected by an electoral college representing a range of interests, the remainder being popularly elected. Even though India has a bicameral Parliament, two members are appointed to the House of the People to represent the Anglo-Indian community. A number of special categories of membership are represented in the National Assembly of Tanzania in addition to the 169 elected members. Fifteen national members are elected by the National Assembly from candidates recommended by mass organisations affiliated with the ruling party, five members are elected by the Zanzibar House of Representatives, 25 regional commissioners sit *ex officio*, 15 members are nominated by the President and 15 seats are reserved for women, the candidates being elected by the National Assembly from a list recommended by the Women's League. Very few countries make specific provision for the representation of women in their Parliaments although many have legal and constitutional mechanisms to protect women from discrimination. In the elections which took place in Pakistan in 1988, 20 of the 237 seats in the National Assembly were set aside for the election of women and another ten for candidates representing non-Moslem minorities. In the National Assembly of Bangladesh, for which elections were also held in 1988, 30 of the 330 seats were reserved for women. In Egypt 30 of the 448 elected members of the People's Assembly must be women and an additional ten seats are reserved for members nominated by the President. In the Soviet Union 75 of the 2,250 members of the Congress of People's Deputies are elected by women's organisations.

In 1987 the Inter-Parliamentary Union published a study of the participation of women in political life which includes, among other information, the distribution of parliamentary seats among men and women as of 30 June of that year. The largest proportions were to be found in the socialist countries. In the Soviet Union 492 of the 1,500 seats comprising the two chambers of the Supreme Soviet were held by women. In China 632 of the 2,978 members of the National People's Congress were women. In Cuba there were 173 out of 510. Among Western countries those of Scandinavia can claim to be the leaders in this field. In 1987, approximately one-third of the members of the Parliaments of Norway, Sweden, Denmark and Finland were women.

In Indonesia 100 of the 500 members of the House of Representatives are appointed by the President. In Malawi the President can appoint any number of members to represent special interests and minorities and enhance the representative character of the National Assembly. In the Philippines 17 members of the National Assembly are appointed by the President, three being cabinet ministers and 14 being representatives of youth, agriculture and labour organisations. In Sierra Leone the 124 members of the House of Representatives include twelve paramount chiefs elected by the tribal authorities and seven appointed by the President. The House of Representatives of

27

The Gambia includes five representatives of the chiefs and eight members nominated by the President in addition to the 35 elected members. In Kenya twelve members are nominated by the President, in Zambia ten and in Gabon nine, one representing each of the nine provinces. In Botswana four of the 39 members of the National Assembly are specially elected or co-opted. In Guyana ten members are elected by ten Regional Democratic Councils and two by the National Congress of Local Democratic Organs. The 70-member Legislative Assembly of Mauritius includes eight 'best losers' appointed after each general election by an electoral commission to balance the ethnic representation. The Chamber of Deputies of Greece includes twelve honorary members nominated by the most successful parties from among the most prominent personalities in their ranks. In Singapore provision is made for the election of up to three non-constituency members should the opposition fail to win at least three seats in a general election. Of the 29 members of Tonga's Legislative Assembly, 9 are directly elected, 9 are indirectly elected and 11 sit *ex-officio*.

The Electoral Mandate

The duration of Parliaments and the chambers which comprise them is variable, as is every other aspect of these widely divergent institutions. At one end of the scale are the House of Lords and the Canadian Senate which are never dissolved. At the other is the United States House of Representatives which runs only two years between elections, thus involving Congressmen in an election campaign which virtually never ceases. Five years or four years is the term of most elective Houses, although in many cases they may be dissolved before their statutory term has expired. Six years is the term in Morocco, Nicaragua, and Sri Lanka and in a few countries, including Australia, Mexico, New Zealand and Sweden, three.[1] In the National Congress of Ecuador the 12 members elected by national vote sit for four years and the 59 elected by provincial vote sit for two years. Some upper Houses have longer terms – for example, US and Australian Senators serve terms of six years and French Senators nine, but they retire in rotation at two-year or three-year intervals, as the case may be. Provision is made in the Australian constitution for the double dissolution of both Houses in certain circumstances, but in the case of certain other upper Houses where members retire in rotation it is true to say that the House as a whole is never dissolved.

What is an electoral system designed to do? Should it produce an assembly in which nearly every shade of political conviction is faithfully represented? If so, then the Scandinavian systems probably

28

come closest to achieving this result. Should it produce an assembly representing broadly based coalitions of political opinion in which the number of seats won may be greatly disproportionate to the number of votes cast? The simple majority system leads to this kind of result. Should it be based on an ideology whereby all political opinion is incorporated within a single party, philosophy or movement? We have seen that such systems can provide the electorate with a choice. Should those elected be representatives or delegates? The proposition stated by Edmund Burke in his famous speech to the electors of Bristol, in which he defined the role of a member as a representative guided by his judgment and his conscience, not as a delegate guided only by the will of his constituents, is debated even to this day. Some systems clearly envisage the role of a member as that of a delegate – for example, the constitution of the Soviet Union expressly states that deputies, among their other duties, shall work to implement their electors' mandates. It is obvious that no member, even under the most finely-tuned system of proportional representation, can possibly reflect all the views of all his or her constituents. Under many political systems party discipline provides the substitute for independent judgement since government stability depends on it. But what about issues of conscience? It is interesting to note that during a major debate on capital punishment which took place in the Canadian House of Commons in 1987, a number of members canvassed the views of their constituents and announced that they would vote in accordance with the will of the majority. On this issue, at least, those members clearly regarded themselves as delegates of the majority of their constituents. There are no right or wrong answers to any of the questions posed above. One electoral system is as good as another provided it is not abused and meets the needs of the society for which it is designed.

Notes

1 At the time of writing, a proposal to extend the term of the Australian House of Representatives to four years is under consideration.

3 Parliament within the Structure of Government

Parliamentary institutions are central to most systems of government but their role within the structure of government varies from country to country. Not only are there differences with regard to their specific powers, but also in the measure of power and influence which each is able to exert within the overall framework of government. In this chapter it will be necessary to consider Parliament's relationship with other institutions of government and the basis on which power is shared in various countries.

In Great Britain and countries with a similar system of parliamentary government the executive is responsible to the legislature and the government looks to the popularly elected House to sustain it in office. In the United States and other countries with a congressional system, the executive and the legislature have distinctly separate powers and the former does not depend on the latter to remain in office. In the USSR the Congress of People's Deputies, designated under the revised constitution as the highest body of state authority, represents the power of the people in a state founded on socialist principles. In the one-party states of Africa the legislature is frequently subordinated to the party and the government. In most of the countries of Latin America the army is an important factor to be reckoned with in the structure of government.

Parliament and the Executive

In the art of government, as in most areas of human endeavour, there is a theory and a practice. Under the British parliamentary system, the cabinet is the supreme policy-making body. The Prime Minister and his or her colleagues are Members of Parliament, answerable to the popularly elected House, and likely to be forced into resignation if unable to command the support of a majority on basic policies and issues of confidence. Constitutionally the executive is subject to parliamentary control. In fact, through the exercise of party discipline, a government winning a majority at the polls is usually able to control the legislature. It is less comfortable in a minority situation, when it is obliged to compromise with the opposition parties; and they, for their part, must exercise judgement in the use of their voting power and share the responsibility of maintaining government stability. It is often mistakenly assumed that under British parliamentary practice a government is obliged to resign whenever it sustains a defeat in the popularly elected House. In fact, the government has a wide discretion in determining what shall constitute an issue of confidence. In Great Britain, between 1974 and 1979, the government of James Callaghan suffered defeats on a number of major issues before resigning after a straightforward vote of no confidence was carried by a majority of one.

In Canada, in 1968, the government was defeated on the third reading of a taxation bill and, instead of resigning, proposed a motion to the effect that the defeat did not constitute an expression of no confidence in the government. The motion was carried with the support of a minor party. A defeat on a single issue will not necessarily unseat a government. Much depends on the nature of the defeat and the circumstances in which the defeat takes place. Most Western European countries are accustomed to government by compromise because their governments are formed from coalitions. In some, such as Italy, these coalitions can prove to be fragile and governments come and go on a regular basis. In others, such as Switzerland, the coalition system has been refined to the point where every major party represented in Parliament is represented in the cabinet and they are forced to govern by compromise. In Switzerland at least, a stable system of government has emerged. Under the British parliamentary system the winning party takes full control and coalitions are rare except in wartime.

In some countries, including Great Britain and those which have adopted the British parliamentary system, cabinet ministers must be members of Parliament either by law or convention. This applies not only in constitutional monarchies such as Australia, Canada and New Zealand, but also in certain countries with constitutional presidencies such as India, Malta, and Trinidad and Tobago. It also applies in certain countries with executive presidencies, including Kenya, Tanzania and Zambia. In countries following the British system the head of state appoints the Prime Minister who is normally the leader of the party holding a majority or the largest number of seats in the popularly elected House, but no formal vote of confidence is required in order to instal the government in office. In certain countries with a constitutional presidency, including Israel, Italy and

Greece, the President appoints the Prime Minister after consultations with the various parties, and the latter, having formed his or her government, must seek a vote of confidence from Parliament in order to be confirmed in office. There are many countries in which membership of the council of ministers or cabinet is incompatible with membership of the legislature. They include Argentina, Brazil, Cyprus, France, Luxembourg, Mexico, Monaco, the Netherlands, Norway, Portugal, Sweden, Switzerland and the USA. In some countries, including Belgium, Denmark, Finland, Greece, Italy, Peru, Spain and West Germany, there is no requirement one way or the other. In Guatemala the President may select his ministers from inside or outside Congress, but if they are congressmen they take leave of absence during the period of their appointment and substitutes are appointed to their seats. In Japan a majority of the ministers including the Prime Minister are required to be members of the Diet. In Bulgaria the Council of Ministers is elected by the National Assembly, both deputies and non-deputies being eligible.

Unlike the British constitution, which produced the modern parliamentary and cabinet systems through a process of historical evolution, the American constitution was tailor-made. Government in the United States is based on a deliberate separation of powers which can also be examined both in theory and in its operation. Under the separation of powers defined in the constitution, the President, the judiciary, and the Congress have well-defined powers designed to maintain a balance whereby no arm of government is too strong or too weak. Experience has shown that the balance of power can fluctuate depending on the political circumstances of the day. It has been seen that a strong President can enforce his will and that a Congress determined to curb the power of the President can enforce its own. In making appointments to the Supreme Court both the President and the Senate have a role to play, so that a President could pack the court with the consent of a compliant Senate, but not otherwise. The President can veto any bill which is sent by Congress for his assent, but the Congress can override his veto by a two-thirds majority of both Houses. Relations between the President and the Congress are likely to be easier when the President's own party controls the Congress. However, the party discipline which under-lies the operation of the British parliamentary system has no place in American politics, so that conflicts can occur nevertheless. It is not the powers themselves which change but the use that is made of them.

There are other countries, apart from the United States, where the President is equipped with a veto power. In Guatemala, for example, the President may exercise a veto which Congress may override by a two-thirds majority. Guatemala's thirteenth constitution, adopted in

1985, was designed to enable the Congress to play a more significant role in the system of government. If the President, without vetoing a bill, simply fails to sign it, Congress has the power to order it published after fifteen working days, in which case it becomes law.

The Role of the Party in the Socialist States and the One-Party States of Africa

If one were to ask the rulers of the Soviet Union where the ultimate power resides, they would undoubtedly answer, 'The people' and point to Article 2 of their constitution. If the same question were asked of the rulers of the United States and other Western countries, the answer would certainly be the same. Although the systems of government are radically different there is an inescapable common denominator underlying the theory of government. In the Soviet Union and other socialist states the Communist Party provides political leadership, socialist principles are constitutionally enshrined and the institutions of government conform to fundamental socialist policies which underlie the social and economic fabric of the nation. Under Western systems of government the political parties compete for the approval of the electorate and control of the institutions of government. In the Soviet Union and other socialist states the elected assemblies perform their functions within a precisely defined constitutional framework based on socialist principles.

There is a joke told in Western countries about the candidate in an election campaign who, at the end of an address to his constituents, declares: 'I have stated my principles and if you don't like them I can change them.' Of this same candidate it has also been said that when he was last seen he was wrestling with his conscience but that fortunately he looked like winning. It is unlikely that such jokes would have any currency in a socialist state because there is no conflict of principle among candidates seeking a mandate from their electors. Candidates seeking election in the Soviet Union are already dedicated to the principles of the Soviet state. Their election campaign is not a battle of ideologies but a bid to serve their communities to the best of their ability in accordance with the fundamental principles of a socialist constitution. The constitution of the Soviet Union has recently undergone important revisions. A Congress of People's Deputies has become the highest body of state authority but the constitution defines the political framework in which it must operate. The Communist Party is the only legal party, although citizens who are not members of the party have always been eligible for election to their Soviets. Under the new electoral law the choice of electors in the nomination of candidates will be greatly widened and the influence of the Communist Party in the selection of candidates is expected to be reduced.

In China the Communist Party, while providing political leadership, is not the only legal party. Eight other parties, referred to as the democratic parties but regarded as patriotic and loyal to the communist state, participate in the political process and are represented in the National People's Congress and other institutions of government. In Czechoslovakia the Communist Party is at the head of a movement called the National Front which incorporates other minor socialist parties together with trade unions and youth organisations. In most of the other People's Democracies the Communist Party sometimes styled by a national designation (e.g. in Hungary, the Hungarian Socialist Workers' Party) leads a coalition of like-minded parties or movements. In Bulgaria most of the 400 members of the National Assembly are members of the Communist Party, but at the time of writing, 98 belong to the Agrarian Union and 26 are non-party. In all these countries the reality of power lies with the party, the representative institutions conform to party policies, but the representation of the people, particularly at the grass roots, is also a reality. Deputies are more concerned with protecting the welfare of the people, implementing programmes and keeping the people informed of what is being done in their interests than with the determination of national policy. However, the constitutional reforms being implemented in the Soviet Union are expected to enhance the role of people's deputies, and it remains to be seen what impact the reforms will have on the Soviets at all levels, including the Supreme Soviet.

At the time of writing significant developments are also taking place in Poland and Hungary. Both countries are contemplating the introduction of multi-party systems, and in Poland the unicameral *Sejm* has been replaced by a bicameral Parliament, both Houses being popularly elected. There is a Senate consisting of 100 members and a more powerful House, which will continue to be known as the *Sejm*, of 460 members, in which the opposition parties will be guaranteed a certain proportion of parliamentary seats, although the ruling party will retain its control. The establishment of a bicameral Parliament is also one of the options being considered in Hungary. The constitutional reforms contemplated in Hungary will also include the establishment of a Constitutional Court to deal with the registration of new parties, the function of the Court being to ensure that the constitutions and programmes of the new parties do not conflict with the provisions of the national constitution. The present Hungarian Parliament has already removed the power of the Presidential Council to legislate by decree and as a result meets more frequently to consider and approve legislation. Although the changes in view in

34

Poland and Hungary are not expected to lead to a radical overhaul of the structure of government, at least in the immediate future, they are nevertheless far-reaching and will strengthen the role of Parliament and widen the scope for the expression of dissent.

The party also plays a dominant part in a number of African countries south of the Sahara, the majority of which are one-party states. Benin, Cameroon, Congo, Côte d'Ivoire, Djibouti, Gabon, Kenya, Malawi, Mali, Mozambique, Sierra Leone, Somalia, Tanzania, Togo, Zaire and Zambia are countries having only one legal political party which is the repository of real power. In these countries the party takes precedence over the legislature and the institutions of government conform to the basic policies decreed by the party. In Africa the one-party system is frequently seen as the answer to tribalism, and the sole legal party is invariably the one which led the country to independence in the first place. Almost all African countries have emerged from a colonial past. Some of them, notably Botswana, The Gambia, Mauritius, Senegal, and, until the recent change-over to a one-party state, Zimbabwe, have shown themselves able to operate multi-party systems successfully. The one-party system is the norm however, and in the African countries of the Commonwealth it is interesting to observe how the political system has been integrated with the parliamentary system inherited from the British. General elections frequently offer a choice of candidates, although all are candidates approved by the party. The Parliaments in some of these countries show a spirited independence, ministers being freely criticised and taken to task. The National Assembly of Zambia has regularly come into conflict with the government-controlled press and has exerted its authority over journalists who, in Parliament's view, have been excessive in their criticism of the nation's legislators. The dominance of the party and the structure of the state are, nevertheless, rarely challenged. One cannot compare these Parliaments with those of the West where political parties are subordinated to the system of government and must campaign for power.

The philosophy of the one-party state in Africa was illuminated by the Hon. Didymus Mutasa, Speaker of the House of Assembly of Zimbabwe, in a speech given at the Eighth Conference of Commonwealth Speakers and Presiding Officers held in New Delhi in January 1986. In the course of his remarks, he said:

> The Party will direct the government because the Party, not the government, provides the policy which emanates from the people. It has their support and loyalty which ties them to the State. The Party integrates the nation by a method that maximizes the opportunity of every citizen to participate on a regular and meaningful basis, in the decision-making process.[1]

One-party states are also to be found in the Arab world, notably in Algeria and Syria, although constitutional reform currently in progress may change the political system in the former country. In the case of Syria the National Progressive Front is a coalition led by the dominant movement, the Ba'ath Party, enshrined in the constitution as the leading party in the state and society. Egypt and Morocco have legislatures in which more than one party is represented, whereas all the seats in the National Assembly of Tunisia are, at the time of writing, held by the ruling National Front, the opposition parties having boycotted the general election of 1986.

Parliament and the Head of State: Monarchies

In considering the place of Parliament within the structure of government some attention must be given to the role played by the head of state in the various systems of government which exist. In the constitutional monarchies of Europe the monarch, in normal circumstances, acts only on advice and the reality of power resides with Parliament and the executive.[2] The succession to the Crown is normally determined by the hereditary factor, although Parliament could have a decisive role to play in circumstances where there was no apparent successor. There have been a number of occasions in the history of England where Parliament has decided most emphatically who should or should not reign. Edward II and Richard II were both deposed by Parliament. Charles I was executed after having been judged guilty of high treason by the House of Commons, constituted as a court by its anti-royalist members. In 1660, eleven years later, the House of Commons restored the Crown to his son, who became Charles II. In 1688 this King's brother, James II, was forced to abdicate and Parliament offered the Crown jointly to the Dutch Prince of Orange, who became William III, and his wife Mary, daughter of James II. In 1701 Parliament adopted the Act of Settlement which disqualifies any successor who is not in communion with the Church of England. In more modern times, Edward VIII was forced to abdicate in 1936 because his conditions for remaining on the Throne were not acceptable to his constitutional advisers. Parliament can modify the royal prerogative by legislation and has frequently done so. It is true that all Acts of Parliament require the royal assent but this has not been withheld since 1707. In those other Commonwealth countries which recognise the Queen as head of state she is represented by a Governor-General who is normally a national of the country concerned and is appointed for a fixed term on the advice of the government of that country.[3] The Governor-General is for all practical purposes the head of state and exercises in the Queen's name the same constitutional functions.

There are very few monarchies in the world outside Western Europe and the Commonwealth. There are in fact six additional monarchies in the Commonwealth itself, namely Brunei, Lesotho, Malaysia, Swaziland, Tonga and Western Samoa, whose rulers are independent of the British Crown. Of these countries, only Malaysia operates a parliamentary system close to the British model. However, Parliament plays no part in the choice of the Supreme Head of State of the Federation *(Yang di-Pertuan Agong)*. Of the thirteen states of the Federation, nine are sultanates, and every five years the sultans elect one of their own number to serve as Supreme Head of State. Other monarchies in the world include Japan, Jordan, Morocco, Nepal, Saudi-Arabia and Thailand. In Japan the Emperor has no political power. Thailand has a constitutional monarchy and the National Assembly is involved in the approval of the succession. Jordan, Morocco and Nepal all have elected assemblies but the powers of their Kings are considerable. In Jordan the King himself appoints the thirty members of the Senate. In Saudi-Arabia the powers of the King are virtually absolute.

Parliament and the Head of State: Republics

Having dealt with monarchies, we must now deal with republics, among which there is a wide variation. In some countries the powers of the President resemble those of a constitutional monarch. In others the President is head of government as well as head of state. Some Presidents are directly elected by the people, some by electoral colleges, and in some countries Parliament itself makes the choice. This does not even exhaust the categories, as there are some countries in which the head of state is more of a collectivity rather than an individual.

Not all of the popularly elected Presidents are heads of government. Those of Austria and Ireland, for example, are not executive Presidents even though directly elected by the people. Most of the other directly elected Presidents, however, are political leaders with significant powers, those of Cyprus, France and Portugal providing Western European examples. Costa Rica, Guatemala, Mexico, Nicaragua, the Philippines, Senegal and Sri Lanka are among other countries having popularly elected executive Presidents. The President of Brazil, formerly elected by an electoral college, will in future be directly elected by the people under the provisions of the 1988 constitution, the next presidential election being due in November 1989. The Presidents of some of Africa's one-party states, including Algeria, Cameroon, Côte d'Ivoire, Gabon, Kenya, Mali, Sierra Leone, Somalia, Tanzania and Zambia are also directly elected but the dominant influence of the party usually ensures there will be only one candidate. The Presidents of Finland and the USA, although nominally elected by electoral colleges, are in practice elected by popular vote since the voters elect delegates who have already pledged their support to a particular candidate. However in the USA, in the case of an indecisive result where more than two candidates were involved, the House of Representatives would determine the issue.[4]

There are a number of countries where the President is elected by Parliament or by electoral colleges, often with a strong parliamentary participation. In some cases the President heads the executive, in others he is a constitutional head of state who appoints the Prime Minister and acts on the advice of his government. The President of Argentina is a strong head of state elected by an electoral college consisting of representatives of all the provinces and other regions of the country. In the tiny state of Nauru, where the President is both head of state and head of government, he is elected by Parliament. The President of Israel is a constitutional head of state elected by the *Knesset*, a candidate requiring at least ten members to support his nomination. Greece, Malta and Trinidad and Tobago, are other countries with a constitutional President whose election is exclusively within the power of Parliament. The President of Zimbabwe, who became head of government as well as head of state at the end of 1987, was also elected by Parliament, but will in future be elected by popular vote. West Germany, which is a federal country, has a constitutional President elected by an electoral college consisting of legislators drawn from both the federal and state assemblies. Italy and the Pacific state of Vanuatu operate a similar system, the electoral college consisting of Members of Parliament and delegates from regional councils.

In Switzerland the members of the Federal Council or cabinet are elected by the Federal Assembly at a joint sitting of both Houses. The Council consists of seven members and the Assembly elects one of the councillors to be President of the Confederation for one year at a time. Members of the Federal Council are disqualified from membership of the Federal Assembly, although the former are usually chosen from among the latter in the first instance. In Yugoslavia the presidency is collective, comprising a member of each republic and autonomous province elected by the respective assemblies together with the President of the League of Communists. The office of President rotates among the presidency members, each serving a one-year term.

Under the amended constitution of the Soviet Union, the Congress of People's Deputies elects the Chairman of the Supreme Soviet who is the highest-ranking official in the state and effectively the head of state. The election is for a term of five years and the same person may not be elected for more than two consecutive terms. The Supreme Soviet will remain a powerful organ of the state, but the Congress of People's Deputies will have certain overriding powers, including the power to revoke legislative acts which run counter to the constitution and to endorse certain appointments made by the Supreme Soviet. It will also have a number of exclusive powers, including the amendment of the constitution, the delimitation of state borders, the formation of new autonomous republics and autonomous regions within the union republics, and the encompassment of guide-lines for the domestic and foreign policies of the USSR.

The authority of the Supreme Soviet extends to executive, legislative, judicial and military matters. It appoints the chairman of the Council of Ministers and confirms the appointment of the other members. It can revoke resolutions and ordinances of the Council of Ministers and form or abolish ministries and state committees on the proposal of the Council. It has various other powers which are referred to later. It no longer elects its Presidium, the composition of the latter being specified in the revised constitution. The Presidium consists of the Chairman of the Supreme Soviet, the First Vice-Chairman of the Supreme Soviet, the Chairmen of the Supreme Soviets of the union republics, the Chairmen of the Soviet of the Union, the Chairman of the Soviet of Nationalities, the Chairman of the Committee of Public Inspection, and the chairmen of the standing commissions of the two chambers and the joint committees of the Supreme Soviet. The Presidium is accountable to the Supreme Soviet, but as is evident from its composition it remains a very powerful body. It convenes the sessions of the Supreme Soviet and organises its work, together with that of the Congress of People's Deputies, and exercises the powers of the Supreme Soviet between sessions. Some of its functions, such as the appointment and recall of diplomatic representatives, receiving the credentials of diplomats accredited to the USSR, the conferment of honours and the exercise of the right of pardon, equip it with the characteristics of a collective head of state with the Chairman of the Supreme Soviet at the pinnacle. Prior to the revision of the constitution the Chairman of the Presidium was the *de facto* head of state. However, it was not until September 1988, when Mr. Mikhail Gorbachev was elected to the office, becoming the first Soviet leader to hold it concurrently with that of Secretary-General of the Communist Party, that it became the leading office in the state in terms of real power.

In most of the other socialist states of Eastern Europe the representative assembly confers wide-ranging powers on a body equivalent to the Presidium of the Supreme Soviet. In Bulgaria the functions of the head of state are performed by the President of the

State Council. The Mongolian People's Republic also has a system following a similar pattern. Variations are to be found in Czechoslovakia where the President of the Republic is elected by the Federal Assembly, and in Romania where he is elected by the Grand National Assembly on the nomination of the Communist Party. Among the functions conferred on the National People's Congress of China by the 1982 constitution is the election of the President and Vice-President of the Republic and other high officers of state. The President appoints the State Council, China's central executive body, on the recommendation of the National People's Congress. In all the socialist states the dominant leadership of the Communist Party ensures that the influence of the party will determine these appointments.

Parliamentary Control of Appointments

One of the checks and balances built into the United States constitution is the power given to the Senate to confirm or reject high-ranking federal officers nominated by the President. They include judges of the Supreme Court, ambassadors and members of the cabinet, together with a wide range of other appointments most of which give rise to no discussion. The power is nevertheless a very real one which the Senate does not hesitate to use in highly controversial cases. Members of the cabinet once confirmed are directly responsible to the President although they may be called before congressional committees to testify in a congressional investigation. The executive power of the President in relation to his cabinet is overriding, as can be illustrated by a story told concerning President Lincoln. Following a major disagreement between himself and his cabinet, he summed up the conclusions of the meeting by saying: 'It appears gentlemen that all except myself are opposed to the resolution before us. It is therefore carried.'

In Peru the Senate appoints or ratifies the appointments of the judges of the Supreme Court, the Attorney-General, the Superintendent of Banking and Insurance, the Comptroller General of Accounts and the highest officers of the armed forces. Magistrates are elected at joint sittings of both Houses. The Senate of Mexico authorises the appointment of ministers, diplomatic representatives, heads of the armed forces and judges of the Supreme Court. The Senate of Argentina enjoys similar powers. In the Soviet Union the Supreme Soviet is empowered to appoint and dismiss the high command of the armed forces and confirm the composition of the Council of Defence. It elects the Committee of Public Inspection and the judges of the Supreme Court, appoints the Procurator-General and the Chief

State Arbiter, and confirms the composition of the Board of the Procurator's Office and the Board of State Arbitration. In Bulgaria the judges of the Supreme Court and the Attorney-General are elected by the National Assembly. In Switzerland both Houses together elect the members of the Federal Council (cabinet), the 30 judges of the Federal Tribunal (Supreme Court) and the nine judges of the Federal Insurance Tribunal. In Portugal the Assembly of the Republic elects the ten judges of the Constitutional Court and other senior judges, the *Provedor de Justiça* (ombudsman), the President of the National Council for the Plan and the members of various public organisations.

Constitutionality of Laws

Some Parliaments enjoy legislative sovereignty. For example, no law duly passed by both Houses of the British Parliament and assented to by the Queen may be challenged in court. It has been said that the British Parliament can do anything by legislation except turn a man into a woman. However, even this is not strictly accurate. If the British Parliament by due passage of an Act of Parliament were to decree that men should be women, then legally, if not biologically, men would indeed be women. The possibility of such a thing happening is hardly to be taken seriously, but the British constitution provides no machinery which could prevent it.

In most countries the actions of Parliament are subject to judicial challenge. In federal states it is normal that both central and state governments should have recourse to the courts should they wish to challenge the constitutionality of a law. Given the division of powers in a federal system the possibility of one level of government encroaching on the jurisdiction of another is always present. In the United States the Supreme Court is the final interpreter of the constitution and, unlike the courts in certain other countries, has never considered itself bound by precedent. In some countries laws may be tested only after they have been adopted, whereas in others a challenge may take place before or during the enactment of a law.

Under some constitutions a special controlling body is set up to oversee the constitutionality of laws. For example, in France all legislation is subject to review by the Constitutional Council, a body vested with considerable powers by the constitution. It consists of nine members appointed for nine years, one third of the membership retiring every three years, the President of the Republic, President of the National Assembly and President of the Senate each appointing three members. In addition former Presidents of the Republic are *ex officio* members. The Constitutional Council oversees the regularity of elections, rules on the constitutionality of organic laws and on any law submitted to it by the President of the Republic, the Premier, the President of the Senate, the President of the National Assembly, or by 60 senators or 60 deputies. It can even pronounce on the regulations of the two Houses of Parliament which are thus not the total masters of their own procedures. In Italy a Constitutional Court of 15 judges performs a similar function. It can decide on the constitutionality of laws, define the powers of the state and regions and determine disputes between them. In Yugoslavia a Constitutional Court consisting of a President and thirteen judges elected by Parliament determines the constitutionality of laws and can stay the execution of an enactment. Proceedings may be instituted by any corporate body or individual, either federally or provincially. Other countries having special constitutional courts include Austria, Egypt, Malta, Poland, Portugal, Spain, Sri Lanka and West Germany.

Some Parliaments monitor their own actions with regard to the constitutionality of legislation. In the Soviet Union the interpretation of laws is a function of the Supreme Soviet. However, the revised constitution also provides for a Constitutional Inspection Committee, to be elected by the Congress of People's Deputies from among specialists in politics and law, whose function is the examination of draft laws to ensure their conformity with the constitution. Its mandate encompasses the decrees of the Council of Ministers and the draft laws of the union republics and decrees of the Councils of Ministers of the union republics. The committee can act on its own initiative, on the instructions of the Congress of People's Deputies, or at the suggestion of the Supreme Soviet, the Presidium, the Chairman of the Supreme Soviet, or the standing commissions and joint committees of the Supreme Soviet. It is also empowered to examine the acts of other state bodies and public organisations, and to table motions in the Congress of People's Deputies, the Supreme Soviet or the Council of Ministers calling for the revocation of instruments found to be in conflict with the constitution.

In the National People's Congress of China all bills are referred to a special committee for examination and report prior to promulgation. The Standing Committee of the National People's Congress has the power to annul an unconstitutional measure. In Hungary also a constitutional committee is appointed by the National Assembly itself. In Bulgaria only the National Assembly may pronounce on the constitutionality of a law, although consideration is being given to the establishment of a Constitutional Court. In Finland the Speaker of the *Eduskunta* and its Committee on Constitutional Law play a part in determining the constitutionality of a law before it is passed. After its passage the President of the Republic may seek an opinion from the Supreme Court of Justice. In Brazil all bills are referred to the

Constitutional and Justice Committee of the Senate at their first parliamentary stage so that a determination can be made as early as possible in the legislative process. Should any law be declared unconstitutional by the Federal Supreme Court, the exclusive power to suspend it in whole or in part belongs to the Senate. A special procedure exists in Thailand which involves the direct and indirect participation of the legislature. Following the passage of a bill, the Prime Minister or one-fifth of the membership of Parliament may seek a ruling from a constitutional tribunal consisting of the President of the National Assembly, the President of the Supreme Court, the Public Prosecutor and four qualified persons appointed by Parliament.

The High Court of Parliament

The powers of Parliament in some countries include other judicial functions. The concept of Parliament as a High Court is rooted in British parliamentary history. In those distant ancestors of the British Parliament, the Anglo-Saxon *Witenagemot* and the Norman *Curia Regis*, the judicial, legislative and executive powers were fused. After the separation of the two Houses in the 14th century it was resolved that the judicial power of Parliament was vested in the House of Lords, and to this day it retains its appellate jurisdiction as the highest court of appeal in the land. Appeals are heard by the Lords of Appeal who consist of the Lord Chancellor and ex-Lord Chancellors, peers who are or have been members of the Judicial Committee of the Privy Council or judges of the superior courts, and a number of other judges known as Lords of Appeal in Ordinary who are specially appointed as life peers in order to hear appeals. When the House of Lords sits as a court of appeal only the active judicial peers normally take part in the proceedings, although the entire House is deemed to be present, and any other peers are entitled to attend should they so desire. Both the House of Lords and the House of Commons act in a judicial capacity when determining questions of privilege, since each House is the judge of matters affecting its own privileges. This principle applies also in many other Parliaments both inside and outside the Commonwealth.

Impeachment

Another judicial power vested in some Parliaments is the right of impeachment. Although it has fallen into disuse in Great Britain, the parliamentary history of that country records numerous cases of impeachment by the House of Commons of ministers of the Crown and others for high crimes and misdemeanours. Persons thus accused were tried by the House of Lords sitting in the capacity of both court and jury. In the United States the impeachment process is by no means obsolete, and might have been invoked against President Nixon had he not resigned in 1974. The constitution provides that the House of Representatives may initiate impeachment proceedings against federal office-holders, including the President, before the Senate which tries the accused person. Judgement extends only to removal or disqualification from office but if a criminal offence is involved the judgement of the Senate does not preclude the launching of criminal proceedings against the person concerned in the ordinary courts of law. Should the President be impeached the Chief Justice of the Supreme Court presides over the Senate for the purposes of the trial. The only President ever to have been impeached was Andrew Johnson in 1868 and the Senate failed by one vote to carry the two-thirds majority required for his conviction.

Many Parliaments possess the power of indictment although its limits and the process involved vary considerably. Brazil, Ireland and Mexico have systems which resemble that of the United States. In India either House could by a two-thirds majority impeach the President and proceed to investigate the charge itself. In certain other countries the trial of an accused person would take place before the Supreme Court or other external tribunal. In Austria both Houses would be involved if the President were charged with violation of the constitution and his trial would take place before the Constitutional Council. In West Germany either House may by a two-thirds majority indict the President for wilful violation of the Basic Law. In France the two Houses acting together could indict the President for high treason and also charge ministers of the government, the trials taking place before the High Court of Justice. In Cyprus three-quarters of the membership of the House of Representatives could indict the President or Vice-President for high treason. In Greece the Chamber of Deputies is empowered to bring charges against the President and members of the government, a trial taking place before an *ad hoc* court presided over by the Chief Justice of the Supreme Court. Côte d'Ivoire, Portugal, South Korea, Spain and Sweden, are among other countries having special impeachment procedures leading to trial by the highest courts in the land. Some Parliaments have special procedures for the indictment of judges. In others, judges and certain other high officials, varying from country to country, may be removed by resolution of the House, or both Houses in the case of bicameral Parliaments, without any impeachment process being involved. In China the power of the National People's

Congress to recall or remove office-holders extends to the highest offices of state.

Parliament and International Affairs

The area of international affairs is one which traditionally has been seen as the preserve of the executive, a domain in which the government rather than Parliament provides the leadership. In Great Britain, as recently as the reign of Queen Victoria, it was even regarded as being within the prerogative of the Crown itself, although by the end of the reign the Crown's advisers had clearly established their own control. There are sound reasons for leaving the initiative in foreign affairs to the executive arm of government. Sudden developments in the international sphere usually call for immediate responses. International negotiations are often complex and sensitive, calling for expert diplomacy and confidential discussion. Parliaments are legislative bodies, and foreign affairs do not normally give rise to heavy legislative loads. However, Parliaments since they represent the people are entitled to be informed of developments in the international field, to debate government policies and actions, and initiate their own investigations of international issues should they so choose. The degree of power and influence exercised by Parliaments in this field varies, but is inevitably limited by the realities of a world dominated by superpowers. Decisions taken by the United States or the Soviet Union affect the whole world, but other countries have no input into the formation of the governments of those colossi. The little man or woman in the world's less powerful countries might be tempted to cry: 'No annihilation without representation!'

Numerous Parliaments are empowered to ratify treaties, usually with certain exceptions, but the extent to which this is a meaningful power would merit a study on its own. In the Soviet Union the power of ratification or repudiation of international treaties is vested in the Supreme Soviet. The constitution of Bulgaria entrusts the supreme guidance of the state's foreign policy to the National Assembly, including the ratification or repudiation of international treaties. In Peru treaties are approved at joint sittings of both Houses. In Mexico this power is vested in the Senate. In Switzerland major international treaties must be submitted to a referendum if this is demanded by 50,000 citizens, and other treaties or agreements may be submitted to an optional referendum if the Federal Assembly so decides. Membership in international organisations such as the United Nations or international communities such as the European Economic Community would be the subject of a compulsory referendum.

In the Western world the body possessing the most significant power in the area of treaties is probably the United States Senate, any treaty negotiated by the President requiring the approval of the Senate by a two-thirds majority.[5] Perhaps the most dramatic exercise of this power was the rejection by the Senate of the Treaty of Versailles after the First World War. The rejection of a treaty after it has been negotiated and concluded by a government is a very serious matter, which is no doubt why those Parliaments which possess the power seldom use it. Many treaties call for consequential legislation which gives Parliament a more decisive role to play, this being equally true in countries such as Great Britain where Parliament has no formal power of ratification. The financial implications of treaties, and indeed of foreign affairs in general, provide opportunities for Parliament to make an input. Debates on the budget and departmental estimates of expenditure can be used to open up questions of policy and administration in the field of foreign affairs. Most Parliaments appoint committees dealing with foreign affairs, and where they are bicameral such a committee is likely to be appointed by each House. They can investigate international and departmental issues, call ministers and their officials as witnesses and produce reports which could in turn provide a basis for further discussion and possible government action. The various procedural devices available to parliamentarians, such as the British-style question period, provide further opportunities for calling ministers to account in the field of foreign affairs as in other areas of government responsibility.

In situations involving states of war and emergency it is again the government which normally takes the first initiative. Most countries have permanent legislation or provisions in their constitutions empowering the government to declare a state of emergency in certain circumstances, and provision is usually made for parliamentary ratification in accordance with procedures which vary from country to country. In Israel, which has been under a permanent state of emergency since its inception in 1948, the *Knesset* renews annually the resolution for its continuation. It is also empowered to extend the application of emergency regulations, or to declare that the state of emergency has ceased to exist. In some countries, including Austria, Malta, Mexico and the United States, the power to declare war is vested in the legislature. However, it has been seen in the United States that it is a power which can be circumvented, since the country became involved in both the Korean war and the Vietnam war without any declaration of war on the part of Congress. United States involvement in the latter war through executive action led to the adoption by Congress of the War Powers Act of 1973 which gives Congress greater control over the commitment of troops abroad.

In the Soviet Union the power to declare war in the event of an armed attack on the country or its allies is one of the many powers vested in the Supreme Soviet, and between sessions, in the Presidium. In Bulgaria decisions relating to war and peace are within the exclusive competence of the National Assembly. While matters of war and peace tend to be matters where the initiative lies with the executive, a government unsupported by the public and its elected representatives would have great difficulty in the successful prosecution of a war. The legislative and financial implications of a declaration of war and conclusion of a peace treaty are far-reaching and the co-operation of Parliament in adopting vital measures and according the necessary powers to the government would be indispensable. Winston Churchill described the Second World War as the unnecessary war because governments and Parliaments around the world failed to take the steps which could have prevented it. International affairs will therefore always be an important area of parliamentary activity even though it is the executive arm of government which should provide the leadership.

Opportunities for individual parliamentarians to work actively in the area of international affairs occur, not only through serving on appropriate committees, but also through membership of international parliamentary associations. Foremost among such associations are the Inter-Parliamentary Union, the Commonwealth Parliamentary Association and the International Association of French-speaking Parliamentarians. These associations organise conferences, seminars and other activities in which parliamentarians from the member-Parliaments participate, thus enabling them to meet their counterparts from other countries, learn of each other's problems and discuss matters of mutual interest. These activities also extend to regional groupings within the associations and bilateral exchanges between Parliaments. Sometimes parliamentarians also have opportunities to attend sessions of the General Assembly and other organs of the United Nations. While these meetings do not result in decision-making, they may sometimes influence the decisions taken by governments. They also provide parliamentarians with an education in international affairs and go far to improving understanding and fostering good relations between countries.

Notes

1 Commonwealth Speakers and Presiding Officers, Eighth Conference, New Delhi, (India), 6–8 January 1986, Proceedings, page 110.
2 The constitutional monarchies of Europe are Belgium, Denmark, Great Britain, the Netherlands, Norway, Spain and Sweden. Liechtenstein, Luxembourg and Monaco fall into a similar category, their heads of state being a Grand Duke in the case of Luxembourg and Princes in the case of the other two.

3 The British Queen is also head of state in Antigua and Barbuda, Australia, Bahamas, Barbados, Belize, Canada, Grenada, Jamaica, Mauritius, New Zealand, Papua New Guinea, St. Christopher and Nevis, St. Lucia, St. Vincent and the Grenadines, Solomon Islands and Tuvalu. There is no state religion in any of these countries and her Governors-General are not subject to any religious qualification.

4 It is possible for an American President to be elected with a minority of the popular vote. Voting takes place on a state basis, and the candidate winning a majority of the popular vote in a state takes all the electoral college votes for that state. The number of electoral college votes depends on the size of the population of the state. Thus, a bare majority of the popular vote in a large state delivers a substantial block of electoral college votes to the fortunate candidate.

5 The ratification power of the Senate does not extend to executive agreements which the President may negotiate with other countries under the authority of specific legislation.

4   Presiding Officers

Any organised meetings require chairmanship, and the role of the presiding officers in Parliaments throughout the world is of crucial importance. Some parliamentary chambers operate under a collective presidency while in others a single individual is vested with complete authority as presiding officer, although he or she is likely to be assisted by deputies. Some presiding officers are political leaders, some are politically active within their parties, some detach themselves completely from their party affiliation and are politically impartial outside as well as inside the House. Some are elected members of Parliament while others are chosen from outside the House. Some are elected by the chambers over which they preside, some are appointed by other methods. In any jurisdiction a considerable prestige is likely to attach to a parliamentary presiding officer and in most cases the duties involve far more than simply presiding over the sittings of the House.

The British Speakership

The historic tradition underlying the office of parliamentary presiding officer is nowhere better exemplified than in the speakership of the British House of Commons. The office of Speaker is almost as old as Parliament itself. The term 'Speaker' derives from the original function of the early Speakers, which was to act as the mouthpiece of the Commons when communicating their resolutions and expressing their grievances to the King. Sir Thomas Hungerford, chosen by his fellow commoners in 1377, was the first Speaker to be so designated, but the origin of the office can be traced back as far as 1258. Its evolution over the centuries has established it as one of great prestige and authority, and today the British Speaker presides over the House of Commons with total impartiality. Invariably a parliamentarian of long experience, he is elected by his fellow-members and sheds his party affiliation as soon as he takes the Chair. He continues to represent a constituency like any other member but does not conduct a political campaign on seeking re-election. The continuity of the speakership and its total political independence are well established conventions in Great Britain. Although the Speaker usually faces opponents at a general election, no Speaker seeking re-election has ever been defeated in his constituency, and since 1835 no Speaker has been ejected from office following a change of government. A Speaker is normally elected in the first instance with the agreement of all parties following consultation, although on two occasions during this century a contested election has taken place. Once elected the Speaker presents himself for the royal approbation. This is purely a formality but is illustrative of the ancient tradition which surrounds the office in Great Britain. The election of the Speaker is always the first business of a new Parliament and if a Speaker dies or retires during the course of a Parliament, a new Speaker must be elected before any further business can be transacted.

The Speaker's duties and authority are derived from custom, precedent and the standing orders. He ensures that the proceedings of the House are properly conducted, maintains order and interprets the rules and practice of the House. He is the traditional guardian of the privileges of the House, which in a modern context can be interpreted as meaning that he protects the right of all members to freedom of speech and the right of all sections of opinion to be heard. He has a particular responsibility towards the protection of minorities, while never losing sight of the rights of the majority. The House looks to him for guidance in matters of procedure; he decides points of order and when required gives rulings which constitute precedents by which future Speakers are guided. The House itself is the master of its own procedure and can change it by resolution, but the interpretations of the Chair have an undoubted impact on the shaping of its practices. The Speaker has a wide range of discretionary powers, enabling him to impose discipline when necessary, deal with procedural abuses and determine whether applications for emergency debates or attempts to raise questions of privilege conform to the necessary criteria. He never takes part in debate and votes only in the case of a tie, in which case he does not take a partisan position but votes in accordance with well-established precedents relating to the casting vote.[1] He also has an important ceremonial role and is the representative of the Commons in its relationships with the Crown, the House of Lords and all external bodies and individuals.

The Speakership in other Commonwealth Parliaments

The speakership in most Commonwealth Parliaments has been considerably influenced by the British tradition, and the powers and duties of Commonwealth Speakers are in many respects similar.

However the real power of the Speaker and the exact nature of his or her role is in practice influenced by the nature of the political system. In Australia, for example, the Speaker of the House of Representatives is an active partisan to whom the rules and practice of the House allow far less discretion than that enjoyed by his or her British counterpart. The rulings of the Australian Speaker are subject to an appeal to the House and in the event of a change of government he or she can almost certainly expect to be replaced. In Canada, although successive Speakers have striven to maintain a tradition of impartiality, only one has ever succeeded in detaching himself from his party and securing re-election as an independent. This particular Speaker, Mr. Lucien Lamoureux, served three terms of office between 1965 and 1974, even though custom had usually decreed that the Speaker change with each Parliament. In 1986 Mr. John Fraser became the first Canadian Speaker to be elected by secret ballot. He was re-elected by the same method in 1988, and it remains to be seen whether this change in the method of election has a permanent influence on the continuity of the office.[2] In India the speakership has been strongly influenced by British practice although few Speakers of *Lok Sabha* have succeeded in detaching themselves totally from their party affiliation. Fortunately the office has been shaped by a succession of strong Speakers both before and after independence and as a result has acquired a reputation for impartiality in the manner of the British model. Indian parliamentarians have tended to place great confidence in their Speakers and look to them for guidance in the development of parliamentary procedure. As a result Indian procedure owes much to the input of Speakers both before and since independence and the discretionary powers of the Indian Speaker exceed those of any other Speaker in the Commonwealth.

In most Commonwealth Parliaments the nomination of the Speaker is regarded as the prerogative of the party in power and if elected for a constituency he or she must expect to fight for the seat like any other member. In some Parliaments the Speaker is not required to be an elected member. This is the case in Guyana, Malaysia, Malta, Singapore, Trinidad and Tobago, several of the smaller Caribbean countries and most of the African Commonwealth Parliaments. In fact in The Gambia, Zambia and Zimbabwe, and also in the Pacific nation of Kiribati, it is specifically provided that the Speaker may not be a member of Parliament. Most Speakers are elected to the Chair by the members of the House, although in many cases this is simply a formal endorsement of a party choice. In Malawi, however, he is appointed by the President of the republic and in Tonga he is appointed by the King. Most Speakers, particularly in one-party states, are active members of their parties and dedicated to their parties' policies. In a one-party state, the traditional conception of the Speaker's impartiality needs to be considered in a different context. Speaker Nabulyato, former Speaker of Zambia's National Assembly, has explained that it 'is judged by the extent to which he avoids being identified with the executive or any particular interest group within or outside the House. It is only an impartial Speaker who can successfully keep at bay the conflicts of responsibility to the House, the party, and other loyalties.'[3]

The Speaker of the US House of Representatives

The speakership of the United States House of Representatives differs in a fundamental way from its British counterpart although it derives from the British office. When the first House of Representatives assembled in 1789, it adhered to the colonial legislative practices with which American legislators were familiar. The colonial Speaker had been a prominent political leader, a popular spokesman in the forefront of the opposition to the colonial government. It was therefore logical that the legislators of the newly independent nation should select their Speaker from among those who had led them in their struggle for freedom. At this period the modern traditions of the British speakership had yet to evolve. The Speaker of the British House of Commons was still an active party leader with an acknowledged political allegiance. With the emergence of cabinet government the British speakership moved towards political impartiality. Once the principle of ministerial responsibility to Parliament had become established, ministers of the Crown became the natural parliamentary leaders of the governing party. The framers of the American constitution, on the other hand, decided that the executive should be separated from the legislature, and it was provided that 'no person holding any office under the United States shall be a member of either House during his continuance in office.' Legislative leadership must be provided however, and in the House of Representatives the responsibility of giving political direction to the majority party devolves in large measure on the Speaker. Thus it is that when the two countries reached the parting of the ways, the two offices began to evolve separately.

The American Speaker is a powerful political leader who is expected to promote the legitimate interests of his party and is certain to be replaced if his party loses control of the House of Representatives. At the same time he is expected to preside with fairness and respect those rules and conventions which protect the rights of the minority. He is entitled to intervene in debate and also to vote, although he rarely does either. At one time he was even more powerful than he is today, and the names of Henry Clay, Thomas B. Reed and Joseph Cannon carry a ring of notoriety to any student of the history of congressional practice. These three Speakers were autocrats who carried their partisanship to extreme lengths.[4] In their day the Speaker was the chairman of the powerful Rules Committee and he also controlled the appointment of legislative committees. These combined powers gave the Speaker a virtually unassailable control over the progress of legislation. In the early part of this century a progressive coalition of congressmen succeeded in carrying a number of reforms which, *inter alia*, debarred the Speaker from membership of the Rules Committee and removed his power to appoint legislative committees. These changes significantly curbed the potential for tyranny inherent in the Speaker's powers prior to their implementation.

The Nature of the Office in Various Jurisdictions

There are few other countries where the Speaker functions as a political leader to the same extent as the American Speaker. There are, on the other hand, numerous Parliaments, even outside the Commonwealth, where the Speaker's role reveals a great deal in common with that of the British Speaker. Great importance is attached to the neutrality of the presiding officers and of their deputies in both Houses of the Japanese Diet and it is not unusual for them to leave their parties following election to the Chair. In most countries, however, a complete severance of party ties on the part of the Speaker would be impractical, and while Speakers are rarely seen to be political leaders they frequently wield considerable political influence. In Israel the Chairman of the *Knesset* is expected to restrict his political activities but is not debarred from returning to active politics. For example, the Prime Minister at the time of writing, Mr. Yitzhak Shamir, was at one time Chairman of the *Knesset*. A Chairman completely divorced from party would have a problem seeking re-election to the *Knesset* because, due to the nature of Israel's electoral system, it is in practice necessary for a candidate's name to appear on a party list in order to secure election as a member. While in office the Chairman of the *Knesset* is expected to preside with complete impartiality in accordance with the practices associated with the British speakership.

An important difference between the duties of the British Speaker and those of his counterparts in countries outside the Commonwealth concerns the planning of the parliamentary agenda. The British Speaker is not involved in the arrangement of business at all, except in certain circumstances where he has a special discretion:

e.g., in the granting of emergency debates or determining the priority to be given to matters of privilege. By contrast, this is a prime duty of presiding officers in many countries, as can be illustrated by reference to the Scandinavian Parliaments. In Denmark, Finland, Iceland, Norway and Sweden, it is the Speaker who convenes the sittings of Parliament, manages the agenda, regulates the proceedings, changes the order of business where necessary, prolongs debate or initiates moves to bring it to a close, and makes arrangements for voting. In Iceland, Norway and Sweden the Speaker may participate in debate and cast a deliberative vote. All Scandinavian Speakers can exert a certain political influence, and it is not unusual for them to have held political office. In Finland and Sweden the Speaker can even find himself or herself participating in the process of forming a government. Should a government fall in Finland, the Speaker is among those who may advise the President with regard to the formation of a new government. Since 1974 the Swedish Speaker has been invested with a status of great constitutional importance. In that year the exercise of the sovereign's prerogatives was transferred to the Speaker, who now plays a central role in the discussions leading to the formation of a government following an inconclusive election. All Scandinavian Speakers are elected by secret ballot and are usually members of the Prime Minister's party except in Finland.

In some Parliaments the presiding officers are elected on an annual basis. This is the case in both Houses of the Swiss Parliament, where continuity in the office would be inconsistent with the Swiss approach to the political power structure. In Peru the Presidents of both the Senate and the Chamber of Deputies are elected annually. In order to be re-elected for a further term an incumbent would require a two-thirds majority of the members present in the chamber concerned. When the two Houses sit jointly as a Congress the two Presidents take turns in presiding.

Collective Presidencies

In a number of Parliaments, the directing authority is a bureau or presidium rather than a single individual. In France the National Assembly elects a bureau consisting of a President, six Vice-Presidents, twelve secretaries who keep the records of proceedings, and three *questeurs* who are responsible for the financial and administrative arrangements of the Assembly.[5] This body of deputies is elected in proportion to the strength of the parties represented in the Assembly. It manages the internal economy of the Assembly and advises the President on matters of procedure and discipline. When the President delivers a ruling he does so with the collective authority of the bureau as a whole. This is of some importance since a ruling cannot be imposed on the Assembly, but a procedural decision backed by the bureau as a whole cannot be lightly disregarded either. The parliamentary agenda is determined not by the bureau itself but by *'la Conférence des Présidents'*, a body which consists of the President and Vice-Presidents of the Assembly, the chairmen of standing commissions, the *rapporteur-général* of the Finance Commission and the leaders of organised parliamentary groups numbering not less than thirty members. The agenda is prepared weekly and must be ratified by the Assembly, although that part of it which is drawn up at the request of the government may not be altered. The Senate also elects a bureau similar to that of the National Assembly but with a smaller membership.

In West Germany the *Bundestag* elects a collective authority known as the *Altestenrat*, which translates literally as the Council of Elders. It consists of the President and four Vice-Presidents of the Assembly and a number of other members representing the political parties in accordance with their relative strengths in the House. Unlike the French bureau, the main function of this body is the arrangement of the programme of business and the allocation of debating time among the various items of the agenda. It also appoints the chairmen of committees. The President of the *Bundestag* has a wider authority and discretion than his French counterpart and his guidance has been a crucial factor in the shaping of West Germany's parliamentary practice since the Second World War. The *Bundesrat* is directed by a body with the emphasis on the representation of the states rather than the political parties. It consists of the President, three Vice-Presidents and an advisory council comprising the leaders of the groups representing each state. The presidency rotates annually among the heads of the various state governments.

In Italy both the Senate and the Chamber of Deputies elect a Bureau consisting of a President, four Vice-Presidents, three *questeurs* and eight secretaries. In order to be elected on the first ballot the President of the Chamber of Deputies requires a two-thirds majority of the total membership. A two-thirds majority is also required on the second ballot, except that blank ballots are counted as affirmative votes. If this is not obtained, an absolute majority suffices on the third ballot. The other members of the Bureau are elected by a simple majority. All parliamentary groups must be represented on the Bureau, and before the voting takes place for the Vice-Presidents, *questeurs* and secretaries, the President consults with the groups in order to promote agreements. The President of the Senate requires an absolute majority to be elected on the first or second ballots, and an absolute majority with the blank ballots being counted as affirmative votes on the third ballot. If the third ballot fails to produce a successful candidate, the two candidates with the largest number of votes compete in a fourth ballot, and in the event of a tie the older of the two is either declared elected or is a candidate in a further ballot. The other members of the Bureau are elected by simple majority, as in the other House, but in the event of a tie between two candidates, the older is declared elected. Under the overall authority of the President, the *questeurs* are responsible for the administration, finances and ceremonial of their respective Houses and the secretaries are concerned with the maintenance of records and the organisation of the proceedings.

Similar collective authorities, some of them combining the features of both the French and West German systems, are to be found in the Parliaments of a number of other European countries including Austria, Belgium, Greece, Portugal and Spain. They are also to be found in some of the African countries schooled in the French parliamentary tradition such as Cameroon, Côte d'Ivoire and Senegal. In Brazil both Houses of Parliament elect a Presidium consisting of the President, two Vice-Presidents, four secretaries and four delegates. In the unicameral Congress of Guatemala a steering committee of twelve members including the President is elected annually. The President may not be re-elected for a successive term and the other members of the steering committee may not be re-elected to the same offices, although a Vice-President, for example, could be elected President.

Presiding Officers in the Parliaments of Socialist States

Under the revised constitution of the Soviet Union the Chairman of the Supreme Soviet is elected by the Congress of People's Deputies and functions as the head of state. The Congress also elects the First Deputy Chairman of the Supreme Soviet. In addition each chamber of the Supreme Soviet elects a Chairman and two Vice-Chairmen, who participate in debate and vote like any other deputy. Joint sittings of both Houses are presided over by the Chairman of the Supreme Soviet or by the Chairmen of the respective chambers on an alternate basis. In China sessions of the National People's Congress are presided over by the Presidium which designates several members to serve as the executive chairmen. In Czechoslovakia the Federal Assembly elects a joint Presidium in addition to those elected separately by each chamber. The Chamber of Nations and the Chamber of the People each elect 20 members to the Presidium of the Federal Assembly which presides over joint sittings, maintains liaison with the Czech and Slovak National Councils and co-ordinates business involving both chambers. In Yugoslavia each chamber elects its own President, and in addition both chambers jointly elect a President and Vice-President of the Assembly as a whole. The President of the Assembly presides over joint sittings and signs decrees on the promulgation of laws. The People's Chamber of the German Democratic Republic elects a number of members to its Presidium in addition to a President and a Vice-President. In Hungary the President of the National Assembly is the directing authority in his own right, while the assemblies of Bulgaria, Poland and Romania elect a small bureau consisting of the President and several Vice-Presidents. In Mongolia the Chairman of the Great People's *Khural* is the head of state.

Presiding Officers of Upper Houses

In some bicameral Parliaments the presiding officer of the upper House is not elected by the chamber over which he or she presides. For example, in Great Britain the Lord Chancellor is the Speaker of the House of Lords, although his functions as a cabinet minister and head of the judiciary are of much greater significance. Unlike the Speaker of the House of Commons he has no disciplinary powers and few procedural functions. He does not rule on points of order, has no casting vote and does not even call on members to speak. As a member of the government he votes in divisions and participates in debate. The Speaker of the Canadian Senate is appointed by the Governor-General on the advice of the Prime Minister, his sole function being to preside over the Senate. Under the rules of the Senate, he has the power to regulate debate, decide points of order and maintain decorum. He has a deliberative vote should he choose to exercise it but no casting vote in the event of a tie.

In the United States the Vice-President of the Republic is *ex officio* the President of the Senate, thereby providing a link between the executive and the legislature. However, his executive duties are of far greater significance than his functions as President of the Senate and he seldom presides in person. A President *pro tempore* is elected by the Senators from among their own number and he, or another Senator designated to preside on an *ad hoc* basis, presides in the absence of the Vice-President. When he does occupy the Chair he never participates in debate and votes only in the event of a tie. He is equipped with certain powers in the regulation of debate but is seldom called upon to exercise them. In Argentina also the Vice-President of the nation is *ex officio* President of the Senate. A similar example is to be found in India where the Vice-President of the Republic is the Chairman of the upper House (*Rajya Sabha*) and a Deputy Chairman is elected by the House to preside in his absence.

Unlike the Vice-President of the United States, the parliamentary functions of the Vice-President of India occupy most of his time. As Chairman of *Rajya Sabha* he is vested with wide powers. He regulates debate, maintains discipline, rules on points of order, protects the privileges of the House, and may even be called upon to interpret the constitution and statutes as well as the rules and practice of the House. His decisions are binding and not open to challenge. He votes only in the event of a tie.

In the upper House of the Austrian Parliament, which has a collective presidency, the office of President rotates in alphabetical order of provinces every six months among members nominated by their respective provincial assemblies. In the Netherlands prior to the constitutional changes of 1983, the President of the First Chamber was nominated by the Crown on the advice of the cabinet. Today he is elected by secret ballot by the Chamber itself.

Presiding Officers in the Order of Precedence

The prestige and dignity of the parliamentary presiding officer are usually recognised by according the office a high place in the national order of precedence. In some cases it ranks immediately after the head of state as in Côte d'Ivoire, Finland, Liechtenstein, Luxembourg, Norway, Portugal, Sweden and Vanuatu. In West Germany the presiding officers of both Houses share second place in the order of precedence, while in Italy the second place is accorded to the elder of the two presiding officers. In the Netherlands the President of the First Chamber takes second place, while in Israel the Chairman of the *Knesset* ranks equally with the Prime Minister after the head of state.

In a number of countries it is a presiding officer who assumes the functions of the head of state in the event of absence, indisposition or a vacancy in the office. In France, West Germany and Italy the President of the upper House is the designated successor. In Trinidad and Tobago it is the President of the Senate followed by the Speaker of the House of Representatives, whereas in Brazil the President of the Chamber of Deputies precedes the President of the Senate in the line of succession following the Vice-President. In Argentina and the United States the President of the Chamber of Deputies and the Speaker of the House of Representatives respectively are third in line following the Vice-President (who is in both cases the President of the Senate). In Austria the President and two Vice-Presidents of the lower House would act for the head of state as a collegiate body, while in Ireland the Chairmen of both Houses would sit together with the Chief Justice as a commission to discharge the necessary responsibilities. In Sweden the Speaker could be called upon to act as temporary regent. Other countries with unicameral Parliaments where the presiding officer could be designated to act as head of state include Congo, Cyprus, Dominica, Egypt, Finland, Greece, Israel, Mali, Papua New Guinea, the Philippines, Portugal, St. Vincent and the Grenadines, Singapore, the Solomon Islands, Tuvalu and Vanuatu.

Women as Presiding Officers

Although the vast majority of presiding officers are and have been men, some Parliaments have on occasion selected women. Canada was one of the pioneers in this field. The first woman to preside over a Commonwealth legislature was Mrs. Nancy Hodges who was elected Speaker of the Legislative Assembly of British Columbia in 1950. Since then two women have been appointed Speaker of the Canadian Senate, and the first woman to be elected Speaker of the Canadian House of Commons, Mrs. Jeanne Sauvé, went on to become Governor-General, the office she holds at the time of writing. Women have been elected to preside over Canadian provincial legislatures on more than one occasion, notably in British Columbia, Manitoba and Prince Edward Island. Elsewhere in the Commonwealth the Speaker of the Australian House of Representatives, the President of the Senate of Belize, the Speaker of the House of Assembly of Dominica, the Deputy Chairman of *Rajya Sabha* of India, the President of the Legislative Council of South Australia and the Speaker of the Legislative Assembly of Himachal Pradesh are currently women. Countries outside the Commonwealth where women are presiding or have since 1980 presided over a legislative chamber include Costa Rica, Iceland, Italy, Norway, Switzerland, Venezuela and West Germany.

Notes

1 The Speaker would normally vote in such a way as to keep the matter open for further discussion or, if this is not possible, to maintain the *status quo*.
2 Other Commonwealth Parliaments where a secret ballot would take place in the event of a contested election for the speakership include Australia, Kenya, Malaysia, Mauritius, Papua New Guinea, Singapore and Tanzania. In New Zealand a secret ballot would take place if the election resulted in a tie.
3 R.M. Nabulyato, The Speakership in Zambia, *The Parliamentarian*, January 1978, vol. LIX, no.1, p.16.
4 A story is told concerning Thomas B. Reed who, when requested by a constituent to provide him with information concerning the rules of the House, responded by sending the inquirer a signed photograph of himself.

5   An interesting tradition is observed when the bureau is elected at the first sitting of the Assembly. The oldest member presides at the election of the President and the six youngest members act as secretaries during the election of the entire bureau. The Italian Senate observes a similar practice when electing its President.

5   Parliaments at Work

Principles of Parliamentary Procedure

The meetings of most if not all corporate bodies are governed by rules of procedure and Parliaments are no exception. The need to provide for the orderly transaction of business is common to every Parliament, and the variations in their practices are perhaps less striking than the wide range of similarities which are to be found among the procedures of the Parliaments of the world. There are no doubt historic reasons for this – the influence of former colonial powers or the dominance of a certain state in a particular region – but there are practical reasons also. To a great extent all Parliaments deal with the same concerns, and parliamentary procedure tends to be complex in any jurisdiction because it must take account of many factors. Although every factor is not necessarily present in every jurisdiction, parliamentary procedure is likely to govern such matters as the passage of legislation, the control of taxation and appropriations, the appointment and operation of committees, the allocation of debating time, the oversight of the executive, and methods of raising grievances. Rules and practices should protect the rights of all members and, where applicable, all parties. They should ensure that all matters can be brought to a decision without at the same time stifling dissent. Opportunities should be available to individual members to raise matters of importance to them and their constituents. In short, procedures should be designed to organise the time of the House in as effective a manner as possible. This does not mean that they should be geared to the principle of maximum efficiency, since this would be inconsistent with free and uninhibited debate. It has been said that the rights of members include the right to waste a certain amount of time, and this is more than just a joke, since in terms of straightforward efficiency an authoritarian regime unhampered by the checks and balances of a representative assembly can usually get things done more readily than a government which can be held accountable.

The nature of parliamentary procedure will be influenced by the political system of which the assembly forms a part. For example, in one-party states it has no need to take account of the confrontational politics on which the systems of most Western democracies are based. In countries where the executive is separated from the legislature the procedures for calling the government to account will differ from those to be found in Parliaments where cabinet ministers are themselves members of Parliament. Custom and convention often play an important part in parliamentary procedure and this certainly applies to British practice which has in turn influenced the practices of many other Parliaments.

British parliamentary procedure may be said to consist of four elements. The traditional practice which has evolved and been refined over the centuries is the basic element and may be described as the common law of Parliament. The principle of financial control by the lower House, the relationship between the two Houses, the various stages through which a bill passes, the relationship of committees to the House as a whole, the role of the Speaker, the quorum of each House (3 in the Lords, 40 in the Commons), the ceremonial, the whole area of parliamentary privilege, are among the matters which form the basic bedrock of practice and procedure. The standing orders are a later procedural development which have codified certain practices, introduced new rules and modified old ones, and imposed restrictions and limitations rendered necessary by the ever-increasing volume of parliamentary business. If traditional practice is the common law of Parliament, the standing orders are analogous to the statute law. The third element is the parliamentary case-law, the precedents arising from the decisions of successive Speakers in interpreting both the traditional practice and the standing orders. Finally there are custom and convention, practices for which no rules are to be found, but which arise from agreements and arrangements which are arrived at to facilitate the passage of business. Where politics are conducted on a confrontational basis, parliamentary procedure provides devices which can be used by both the majority and the minority, enabling the former to expedite its business and the latter to delay or obstruct it. The system will normally allow the majority will to prevail while permitting full expression of minority opinion. A veteran British M.P., Sir Bernard Braine, writing in the House Magazine (the weekly journal of the British Houses of Parliament) in 1987, had this to say: 'Not being able to take the House for granted helps to keep ministers on their toes and is essential to the health of parliamentary democracy.'

American congressional procedure differs markedly from British parliamentary practice although both share a common heritage. The first codification of congressional procedure was Jefferson's Manual, which remains a standard work and illustrates the common origins of the two systems. Today, however, to quote from a valuable comparative work, 'the two are separated by a width of incomprehension, an Atlantic of the mind, which prevents each from benefiting from the acquired wisdom of the other.'[1]

This divergence was brought about by the separation of powers on which the American system of government is based. Congressional leadership is very different from parliamentary leadership because members of the executive have no place in Congress whereas they are the leaders of the majority, or at any rate of the party forming the government, under the parliamentary system. Power under the congressional system is more widely distributed. The bulk of the legislation dealt with by Congress is unlikely to be initiated by the executive, whereas the reverse is the case in a British-style Parliament. The evolution of Congress over the past two centuries has led to the adoption of procedures designed to deal with a variety of situations. In the House of Representatives the Rules Committee plays a major part in determining the progress of a bill on the floor of the House, after it has emerged from the committee dealing with it, and the reports of the Rules Committee enjoy a privileged status. There are also methods of expediting the passage of a bill, and the various procedures which could be employed add up to a system of considerable complexity.

Both Houses of the British Parliament and the United States Congress exercise total control over their rules of procedure, but this is not the case in all Parliaments. In France the rules of both Houses are subject to the approval of the Constitutional Council, and there are a number of other countries where Parliament's rules could be subject to the intervention of the Supreme Court or other extra-parliamentary body. In some countries certain requirements concerning the conduct of parliamentary business are specified in the constitution. This is so in the case of the Soviet Union. It is also the case in some western countries including France. Even in Canada, a country which has adopted the British parliamentary system, the constitution provides for certain aspects of the conduct of parliamentary business: for example, the House of Commons quorum of 20 members is a constitutional requirement.

Languages Used in Parliaments

The proceedings of a Parliament are conducted by means of debate leading to a vote. Most countries have only one official language, but there are some bilingual and multilingual countries where more than one language will be heard in the course of parliamentary debate. Language questions can be politically divisive issues, so that a unilingual Parliament has one less potentially controversial issue to contend with than those where more than one language is spoken. Furthermore, bilingual and multilingual Parliaments incur heavier administrative costs because of the need (felt by most of them) to publish official documents in more than one language and, in the case of Parliaments where it is provided, the provision of simultaneous interpretation of parliamentary debates.

Bilingual Parliaments where simultaneous interpretation is available include Canada (French and English), Cameroon (French and English), Senegal (French and English, the latter having been introduced following the confederative union of Senegal with The Gambia) and Belgium (French and Flemish). In the case of Belgium, German is also used in Parliament on occasion, even though it is not an official language. The languages of the Israeli Parliament are Hebrew and Arabic, simultaneous interpretation being provided from Hebrew into Arabic. Irish Gaelic is the official language of Ireland although English is the language of common usage. Simultaneous translation is available in the lower House from Irish into English. In Finland, where a minority of the population is Swedish-speaking, both Finnish and Swedish may be used in Parliament but no simultaneous translation is provided. Other bilingual Parliaments where simultaneous translation is not usually available include Czechoslovakia (Czech and Slovak), the Philippines (English and Filipino), Kenya (English and Swahili), Tanzania (English and Swahili), Malta (Maltese and English, the former being the official language), Nauru (English and Nauruan) and South Africa (Afrikaans and English). In Mauritius the official language is English although French and Creole are also widely spoken.

Turning now to multilingual Parliaments we find that simultaneous translation facilities are provided in all cases dealt with below. India is a country of many languages although only two, Hindi and English, are recognised as official at the national level. Sixteen regional languages, including Hindi, are recognised in the constitution, but the languages normally used in the central Parliament are Hindi and English. Use of another language requires the permission of the presiding officer. Yugoslavia has a number of national languages, the principal ones being Serbo-Croatian, Slovenian and Macedonian, and these are the languages of the federal legislature. Switzerland's three official languages, German, French and Italian, are all spoken in the federal Parliament. A fourth language, Romansch, is a national but not an official language. Sinhala is the official language of Sri Lanka but Tamil and English are also used in Parliament. Singapore has four official languages, English, Malay, Mandarin and Tamil, all of which may be spoken in Parliament although English is the dominant language and the debates are published in English only. The Pacific nation of Vanuatu, formerly the New Hebrides, and an Anglo-French condominium, inherited both English and French from the colonial powers and together with the indigenous language, Bislama, has three official languages. The principal language used in the Congress of People's Deputies and the Supreme Soviet of the USSR is Russian although deputies representing other nationalities may also speak in their national languages. In China the language of the overwhelming majority is Chinese (Han) but the six minority languages may also be used in the National People's Congress.

In most African countries south of the Sahara, so many languages and dialects are spoken that the language of the former colonial power is frequently the only practical language for use in Parliament. An exception is Tanzania where, because Swahili is spoken through-out the country, it is the major parliamentary language. Indigenous languages are also employed in certain other African Parliaments. For example, Shona and Ndebele are used in both Houses of Zimbabwe's Parliament, although English is the principal language of debate. Papua New Guinea, a country in the Pacific region, has over 750 languages, many of them mutually unintelligible even though derived from common roots. The nearest thing to a common language is pidgin, a corruption of English, and is the ·language spoken in Parliament. English is spoken by a small minority of the population but it may one day become the national language with the continuing spread of education. In the Solomon Islands both English and pidgin are official languages.

The Legislative Process

General Principles

A major function of any Parliament is the making of laws; in fact, the terms 'parliament' and 'legislature' are often used synonymously. A draft law, which is usually referred to as a bill, can take various forms and deal with a wide variety of subjects. It can be an original piece of legislation or it can propose to amend or repeal an existing law. In the course of its passage it is itself subject to amendment. In some countries certain bills, such as those seeking to amend the constitu-tion, are subject to special procedures, sometimes involving popular referenda as in Australia and Switzerland. In the United States Congress joint resolutions, when agreed to by both Houses in identical form, have legislative effect. They are usually employed for minor legislative purposes, in which case they differ little from bills.

However, they retain one important function in that all amendments to the constitution are proposed in this form and when adopted are sent to the states for ratification, the approval of three-quarters of the state legislatures being required. In most jurisdictions the adoption of a measure by a legislative chamber usually requires a simple majority. However, in most countries certain measures, such as those proposing to amend the constitution, require the approval of a more substantial number of members, such as a two-thirds majority, and in some cases even more.

A bill can be initiated in various ways. The executive plays an important role, and in many countries the dominant role, in initiating legislation. Individual members of Parliament may initiate legislation, subject in some countries to certain restrictions. Under the revised constitution of the Soviet Union legislation may be initiated by deputies in the Congress of People's Deputies and in both chambers of the Supreme Soviet. In some Parliaments, bills may be initiated by parliamentary committees, and this is common in the socialist states. Finland, Israel, Japan and Sweden are among other countries where parliamentary committees may in certain circumstances initiate legislation. In Finland this right is limited to two committees, the Finance Committee, which may propose tax bills, and the Bank Committee, which may propose changes to the law governing banks. In some countries extra-parliamentary bodies have the right to initiate legislation, and again this is a practice not uncommon in the socialist states. In the Soviet Union the Supreme Court, the Procurator-General, the Committee of Public Inspection, the Chief State Arbiter, the Academy of Sciences and the union bodies of public organisations are among the bodies which enjoy this right. A variety of judicial and political bodies and public organisations are similarly privileged in Bulgaria, China, Cuba, the German Democratic Republic, Mongolia and Romania. In Italy the regional councils, municipal councils and the National Council for Economy and Labour may initiate legislation. In Guatemala the Supreme Court and the National University may do so. Regional assemblies are accorded this right in Finland and Portugal and, in the former country, the Evangelical Lutheran Church may propose bills to change the ecclesiastical law. In Great Britain measures framed by the General Synod of the Church of England may be submitted to Parliament, where they are considered by the Ecclesiastical Committee composed of members of both Houses, prior to being adopted. There are certain federal countries, including West Germany, Mexico, Switzerland and Yugoslavia, where the component states may initiate legislation at the federal level. In the Soviet Union the union republics may do so through their highest bodies of state authority.

In some countries bills may originate by popular initiative. For example, in Austria 100,000 voters or one-sixth of the voters in three provinces may initiate a legislative proposal. In Italy 50,000 electors may do likewise. Cuba's constitution provides that such an initiative may be taken by 10,000 citizens. In Liechtenstein 600 electors or three parish councils may initiate legislation, these numbers being increased to 900 and four respectively in the case of proposals to change the constitution. In Switzerland 100,000 citizens may initiate a constitutional proposal but there is no provision for the introduction of ordinary measures by popular initiative.

In countries with bicameral Parliaments the legislative function is shared by both Houses. However, there are few countries in which the powers of the two Houses are exactly the same, Belgium, Czechoslovakia, Italy, the Soviet Union, Switzerland and Yugoslavia, being among the exceptions. It is generally the case that bills, other than financial bills, can originate in either House but again there are exceptions. The Parliaments of Austria, Jordan, the Netherlands, Spain and Thailand are among those where all bills must commence their passage in the lower House. There are many countries where the initiative in financial matters is reserved to the lower House, and in this regard British parliamentary practice has been a significant influence. Parliaments were originally summoned by the mediaeval Kings of England because they needed money, and since the main burden of taxation fell upon the Commons (as the representatives of the cities, towns and counties came to be known) the initiative in matters of grants and taxation was conceded to them very early in English parliamentary history. Today the financial supremacy of the House of Commons is total. Although the House of Lords retains the theoretical right to reject a money bill, to do so would have little effect. The Parliament Acts of 1911 and 1949 severely curtailed the powers of the House of Lords and reduced their ultimate power over legislation to one of delay. They could delay a money bill for one month and any other bill for one year (with the exception of a bill affecting the duration of Parliament which would be exempted from the provisions of the Acts).

Although there are only a few other countries where the supremacy of the lower House is almost total, the financial initiative is reserved to the lower House in the majority of bicameral Parliaments. All the bicameral Parliaments of the Commonwealth observe this practice, even in Australia where the Senate is popularly elected. In the United States all revenue-raising bills must originate in the House of Representatives and, by custom, all general appropriation bills as well. Otherwise the financial powers of the Senate are equal to those of the lower House. Argentina, France, Ireland and Mexico are among other countries where the financial initiative is reserved to the lower House. In France the National Assembly has the power of final decision on most matters, and in Ireland the legislative power of the upper House is restricted to one of delay as in the House of Lords. In West Germany a budget bill once adopted by the *Bundestag* does not require the formal consent of the *Bundesrat*. In Austria the *Nationalrat* has exclusive jurisdiction over all financial legislation and simply communicates its decisions to the *Bundesrat*. The *Nationalrat* can also override the veto of the *Bundesrat* in respect of other bills except those seeking to amend the constitution or limit the legislative and executive powers of the provinces and those affecting the *Bundesrat* itself.

In the Soviet Union both Houses of the Supreme Soviet have equal powers, but each has priority concerns assigned to it. Questions of social and economic development and of the development of the state as a whole, the rights, freedoms and duties of citizens, foreign policy, defence and state security are matters of special concern to the Soviet of the Union. Questions of social and economic development of the republics, autonomous regions and autonomous areas, national culture, inter-ethnic relations and ethnic equality are the special concerns of the Soviet of Nationalities. In Yugoslavia, where both Houses also enjoy equal status, each has its own defined sphere of competence. Where financial matters are concerned, the Federal Chamber adopts the budget, while the Chamber of Republics and Provinces decides the total level of expenditure. In summing up it may be stated as a general principle that both Houses in a bicameral Parliament must agree to a measure in order for it to become law. One House may propose amendments to a bill sent to it by the other House, which in turn must be further considered by the House originating the measure. In many countries provision exists for conferences between the two Houses in cases of conflict. Unless there is a mechanism whereby the will of one House may prevail over that of the other, a bill on which no agreement can be reached must fall.

British and Related Practices

In some countries, as we have already observed, the legislative programme is largely controlled by the executive, this being the case in Great Britain and other countries operating the British parliamentary system. Most of the time available for legislation is at the government's disposal in the Parliaments of these countries, although any member has the right to introduce a bill. A limited amount of time is usually made available for the business of private members or backbenchers, the terms used to describe members who do not hold government office, but their bills rarely reach the statute book. Ballots are held in some Parliaments to determine the members

68

whose bills or motions should be brought before the House for debate, and successful members usually consider themselves lucky to obtain a debating opportunity, even though there is no guarantee that the measure concerned will be brought to a vote. Under British practice only the government can initiate bills proposing expenditure or taxation, and this imposes a severe limitation on the kind of legislation which can be initiated by private members. Even bills with incidental financial implications cannot proceed unless the government is prepared to furnish the necessary recommendation respecting those provisions.

Government bills are likely to pass through a number of pre-consideration stages before they are introduced into Parliament. They will probably have originated in a government department and will certainly have been considered in cabinet. In many cases there will probably have been an input from outside bodies and experts with an interest in the subject of the legislation. Further public input is possible in the course of a bill's passage: for example, depositions might be submitted or witnesses called to give evidence before a committee considering the bill. A session of a British-style Parliament will usually open with a speech delivered by the head of state outlining the government's programme and legislative intentions for the session. The first business of the session is likely to be a wide-ranging debate on the content of the speech, during which amendments can be moved to the motion before the House concentrating debate on particular aspects of government policy, often leading to votes expressing confidence or non-confidence in the government.

Bills pass through a number of stages comprising three readings and a committee stage, and sometimes a separate report stage when a bill is returned to the House from a committee. The first reading is a formal stage involving simply the bill's introduction, no debate taking place. It is interesting to note that the Canadian House of Commons has maintained a practice, largely abandoned in Great Britain, whereby the minister or member presenting a bill first moves for leave to introduce it. This is no longer a debatable motion, although a member will sometimes use the opportunity to make a brief statement describing the purpose of the bill.

The second reading is the stage at which the main debate takes place on the principle of the bill. If adopted at this stage, it is then referred to a committee, which could be a committee of limited membership or a committee of the whole House. Practices vary even in Parliaments operating the same system. In small Parliaments all bills are likely to be referred to committee of the whole, whereas in larger Parliaments such as those of Great Britain and Canada the majority are likely to be referred to specially constituted legislative committees. The committee of the whole has no place in India's parliamentary procedure and all bills are considered in smaller committees. The committee stage is the stage at which a bill is given detailed study on a clause-by-clause basis, and in some jurisdictions, legislative committees are empowered to summon witnesses. In some Parliaments a report stage may follow the committee stage, this being the practice in Great Britain and Canada. It is a stage at which amendments adopted or rejected in committee may be reconsidered and further amendments moved. The final stage in a bill's passage is the third reading, when the final text of the bill, incorporating any amendments which have been adopted, can be further debated. In a bicameral Parliament a bill agreed to in one House is referred to the other where it goes through a similar process. Once adopted it becomes law as soon as the required formalities and promulgation procedures have been observed.

The US Legislative Process

In the United States Congress the right to introduce a bill is restricted to Senators and Congressmen. A considerable proportion of legislation is nevertheless initiated by the executive, although such a bill must be introduced in the name of a member. A bill emanating from the executive is communicated to the Speaker of the House of Representatives who will refer it to the committee having jurisdiction over the subject. Such a bill is customarily introduced in the name of the chairman of the committee concerned. Under the congressional system individual members have far more scope and opportunity for introducing their own bills than under the parliamentary system. The same considerations of party discipline and solidarity do not apply. The incentive for sponsoring a particular bill may be determined by the member's personal stand on a specific issue, by the particular needs of the member's state, district or constituents, or by the activities of a pressure group to which a member wishes to respond. Although there are time constraints, and a bill can face many hurdles, the legislative programme is not dominated by the demands of the executive as under the parliamentary system. A bill must be agreed to by both Houses in order to be adopted and provision exists for conferences between the two Houses in cases of deadlock. A bill once adopted must be sent to the President for his approval and he has the right of veto which must be exercised within ten days (Sundays excepted). However, a presidential veto can be overturned by a two-thirds majority vote in both Houses.

In both the Senate and the House of Representatives, unless the House concerned suspends its rules, every bill must be considered by the committee having jurisdiction over the subject before it can make any further progress. Normally a series of hearings will be held by the committee or a sub-committee, and in due course the bill will be reported, with or without amendments, or the committee may decide not to proceed with it, in which case it is effectively killed. It is not unusual for a committee to consider simultaneously more than one bill on the same subject, in which case the bill which finally emerges is likely to be the committee's own version. The procedures to which a bill is subject once reported from a committee can vary considerably, and in the House of Representatives the Rules Committee plays a decisive role in determining the procedure to be adopted. The committee must first be satisfied that the bill should go forward and will hear the sponsor of the bill and the chairman of the committee reporting it before making a decision. It may then propose a rule allocating debating time, or it may propose a 'closed' rule, which has the effect of disallowing amendments except by the committee reporting the bill. The Speaker automatically recognises the chairman of the Rules Committee whenever he offers a report. A bill involving expenditure or taxation will be taken in committee of the whole House before being reported to the House itself, where the final passage of a bill is determined. In spite of the complexities of congressional procedure there are various ways of expediting the passage of a bill, and the majority of bills adopted are disposed of through the use of time-saving devices.

Further Examples of the Operation of the Legislative Process

In Japan a bill may be introduced by a member of either House of the Diet, by the cabinet or, in the case of highly specialised bills, by a committee. To introduce a bill a Diet member requires the support of at least 20 members of the House of Representatives or ten members of the House of Councillors, these numbers being increased to 50 and 20 respectively in the case of bills affecting the budget. In practice all Diet-originated bills are sponsored by a political party. A cabinet bill will originate in a government department and will be introduced by the Prime Minister in one House or the other. A bill originating in a committee will have been negotiated and agreed to by all the parties involved and will be introduced by the committee chairman. Most of the bills introduced and adopted originate with the government, although a considerable number of Diet-originated bills also reach the statute book. The final decision with respect to the adoption of a law rests with the Diet and there is no veto procedure.

In Switzerland the executive and the legislature work closely together in the initiation and passage of legislation. The members of the Federal Council (the cabinet) may not be members of the Federal Assembly, but they regularly attend and speak in one or other of the two chambers and their committees. A bill may originate in either

House of the Federal Assembly on the initiative of any member, or it may be proposed by the Federal Council, or it may be requested by a canton. The Federal Council is usually asked to provide a report on the proposed measure and the two Houses will agree as to which of them will first deal with it. It will be subject in both Houses to committee study followed by general and detailed debate, and even if agreed to by both Houses, there may yet be a further process. In cases of disagreement between the two chambers, provision is made for a meeting of conciliation involving members of the committees which originally dealt with the bill. Both Houses may initiate motions which, if adopted, oblige the Federal Council to take certain measures. One kind of motion, known as a 'postulate', may be submitted by either House independently of the other and will call forth such response as the Federal Council deems appropriate. In Switzerland a distinction is made between laws and decrees, although both are passed in the same manner and have equal force in law. Laws, which are always of universal application, may be submitted to a national referendum if demanded by 50,000 voters or eight cantons within 90 days. Decrees are not similarly liable unless they too are of universal application.

Committees play an important part in the legislative process in most Parliaments, and under the congressional system a committee can decide the fate of a bill. There are a number of Parliaments where a bill is referred to a committee before it is even considered in the House itself, a practice which reinforces the role of committees by giving them the initiative of leadership at the outset of a bill's passage. Countries where initial study of legislation takes place in committees include Argentina, Brazil, Côte d'Ivoire, France, Greece, Guatemala, Italy, Japan, Luxembourg, Mexico, the Netherlands, Norway, Portugal, Sweden and Switzerland.

In the West German *Bundestag* a bill goes through three readings, consideration in committee taking place between the first and second readings. A general debate may take place at first reading, but very often a bill is referred directly to a committee without debate. Detailed examination takes place in the House at second reading when amendments may be proposed. Third reading debate is limited to those clauses to which amendments have been proposed. The process is similar in the Austrian *Nationalrat*, where the bulk of legislative work is done by committees. The second reading debate is based on the committee's report, and consists of a general debate opened by the committee's rapporteur, followed by a special debate, although they are normally held as one. The third reading is the stage at which drafting details are tidied up and a vote is taken on the text in its entirety. In both Houses of the National Assembly of Thailand the stages of a bill also consist of three readings, the principle being considered at the first reading before it is referred to committee. The second reading is the stage at which it is considered in committee and reported to the House for further consideration. A bill is normally considered in a committee appointed by the House, but it can be referred to a committee of the whole at the request of the Council of Ministers or on the adoption of a motion seconded by at least 20 members in the House or 30 in the Senate. No debate takes place at the third reading. In countries where the British parliamentary system operates, the House debates and determines the principle of a bill before it is referred to a committee (which may be a committee of the whole House) and the committee is bound by the principle of the bill to which the House has agreed. It is true that a bill could be disembowelled by the defeat of a key clause, but an amendment adopted in committee can always be reversed in the House itself.

The Legislative Process in Socialist Countries

In the socialist countries the legislative process needs to be considered in the context of a different political system. The radical changes which are taking place in the Soviet Union at the time of writing will undoubtedly have an impact on the legislative process. The new Supreme Soviet is expected to hold two sessions a year of three or four months duration and have a greater involvement in the enactment of legislation prior to final ratification. At the same time it is expected that the standing committees will continue to be as active as before. The pre-reform Supreme Soviet was more like a delegate conference than a Western-style Parliament. Although it always had the ultimate power of decision and ratification, its permanent organ was the Presidium, which provided continuity between sessions and exercised extensive delegated powers. Under the revised constitution the Presidium will remain a very important body exercising the authority of the Supreme Soviet when the latter is not in session.

The right to initiate legislation is spread widely. A bill can originate in the Congress of People's Deputies, in either chamber of the Supreme Soviet, its Presidium, the Council of Ministers, the Union Republics, joint committees of the Supreme Soviet and standing committees of either House, with the Chairman of the Supreme Soviet and with individual deputies; and as we have already seen, the legislative initiative extends to the judiciary and public organisations. Standing committees can determine their own agendas, undertake inquiries within the area of their mandate and present draft bills for the consideration of the Supreme Soviet. Much of the preparatory work in framing legislation has in the past been undertaken by the standing committees so that draft laws had been thoroughly aired and thrashed out in detail before they reached the Supreme Soviet which, prior to the recent reforms, never remained very long in session. The work of the standing committees will undoubtedly continue to be of very great importance under the reformed system, but legislafion is likely to receive more detailed consideration in the Supreme Soviet itself. The constitution stipulates that a law of the USSR must be passed by a majority of the total number of deputies in each chamber, although other decisions may be adopted by a simple majority of the members present. In the event of disagreement between the two chambers, provision is made for negotiation through a conciliation commission comprising an equal number of members from both chambers followed by consideration of the measure at a joint sitting. In the event of failure to agree the matter is submitted for the consideration of the Congress of People's Deputies.

In Bulgaria, where constitutional reform is also under consideration, a new programme for the development of socialism emphasises the primacy of the National Assembly in which permanent standing committees will continue to play a crucial role. They, together with the Council of Ministers, the Supreme Court, the trades unions and other public organisations, can initiate legislation. All bills receive thorough consideration in the committees, after which they are further considered by the Assembly itself. Amendments can be moved, proposals may be entertained from members of the public, and the bill may be referred back to the committee for re-consideration. Every draft law is submitted to the Assembly for two votes and once adopted it cannot be vetoed.

In China the legislative initiative is also spread widely, but the need to legislate would appear to be less frequent than in Western nations. The constitution is specific with regard to the principles on which government must be conducted, and there is likely to be a legislative initiative only when the leading organs of government deem it necessary to codify or clarify certain principles. The National People's Congress is the highest body of state authority. It meets regularly but does not remain in session for lengthy periods. It has the ultimate power of decision and ratification, continuity between sessions being provided by its Standing Committee, which is its permanent organ. The Standing Committee has wide-ranging powers and its decrees have equal force in law as the laws enacted by the National People's Congress itself.

A bill may originate with the National People's Congress, its Presidium (collective presidency), its Standing Committee, various special committees, the State Council, the Central Military Commission, the Supreme People's Court and the Supreme People's Procuratorate. All bills put forward are submitted for examination to delegations of deputies and special committees which report to the Presidium or, when the National People's Congress is not in session, to its Standing Committee. The Presidium or the Standing Committee, as the case may be, may in their discretion submit bills to the general session of the National People's Congress for voting, which may be carried out either by secret ballot or show of hands.

Importance of the Legislative Function

It is not within the scope of this book to describe the many variations in the legislative process which are to be found throughout the Parliaments of the world, but we hope that the examples cited will provide some idea of the extent of these variations. Some commentators, including Walter Bagehot writing in the last century on the English constitution, have expressed the view that law-making is no longer Parliament's most important function. It is a view encouraged by the fact that in so many countries the executive controls the legislative programme and can usually secure most of its measures. An author writing about the French Parliament has warned against placing too much emphasis on this view, however.[2] In France the government for all practical purposes controls the legislative activities of Parliament, and enjoys prerogatives which include the power to call for a block vote on a controversial measure. A block vote has the effect of preventing the House from voting separately on proposed amendments and allowing only a single vote on the text as a whole. In spite of this the author attaches great importance to the legislative function of Parliament, pointing out that parliamentarians know better than the bureaucrats what the public is prepared to put up with. He also points out that the experts are not confined to the framers of government measures. There are experts in many fields also represented in Parliament. The revolutionary declaration that 'the law is the expression of the will of the people' may be a little starry-eyed, but it is vital that there should not be too great a distance separating the government from the governed. Parliaments exist to provide that bridge.

Financial Control and the Budgetary Process

British and Related Practices

The oversight of the budget is at the heart of any parliamentary system. The need to raise revenue is closely associated with the origin of popular representation, as can be illustrated by reference to British parliamentary traditions. As we have seen, Parliaments were originally summoned by the mediaeval English Kings because of their need of money, and the right to raise grievances before granting supply (i.e., the money required to supply the needs of government) became the basis of financial procedure. In theory this principle has never been totally abandoned, although public finance is today so complex that it is idle to pretend that parliamentary control over finance is anything like 100% effective. Great Britain is no longer governed by autocratic monarchs. The direction of affairs is in the hands of a government elected by the people, and since modern governments are involved in virtually every area of public activity their financial needs are extensive. Parliamentary approval is required for all expenditure and taxation. Parliament also determines the appropriations – i.e., the allocation of funds to the various government departments, agencies, programmes and projects – but it does so on the basis of proposals put forward exclusively by the government. No expenditure may be proposed unless sanctioned by the government's recommendation. The estimates of expenditure are prepared by the government and the necessary recommendation is signified by the Queen in her speech opening a session of Parliament. Any other measures involving expenditure require a separate recommendation. Taxation measures are based on ways and means resolutions which can only be introduced by a minister. In Britain the taxation structure requires to be renewed every year and for this purpose an annual Finance Bill is introduced each session, incorporating any new or amended taxation proposals. The government normally relies on its majority to carry its measures, so that in realistic terms executive power has encroached considerably on the traditional powers of Parliament.

However, Parliament's financial control, while much reduced, is far from being a myth. Although handicapped by limited opportunities for detailed study, procedures are in place which ensure that the House of Commons retains its oversight function in a meaningful way. A major debate lasting several days always takes place following the budget statement of the Chancellor of the Exchequer. It is a wide-ranging debate covering many issues, since the entire budgetary structure is open to discussion. New taxation proposals, existing taxation and the expenditure for which they are designed, together comprise a complete scheme of revenue to be debated as a whole, so almost all matters concerning the responsibilities of government would fall within the scope of the debate.

Another opportunity for broad debate occurs at the second reading of the Finance Bill. Although narrower in scope than the budget debate, a general review of national finance normally takes place, and detailed consideration of the bill takes place in committee. Under current practice the bill at this stage is divided between a committee of the whole House and a standing committee.[3] With regard to the estimates of expenditure, it has long been recognised that thorough consideration in the House of the spending requirements of all government departments is totally impractical. Since 1979 a select committee structure has been in place whereby fourteen of the total number of committees are charged with the oversight of government departments. Each has a specific subject mandate and they examine, among other things, the estimates of the various departments within their separate subject areas. They can present reports to the House and opportunities exist, albeit limited, for debating these reports on the floor of the House itself. Three days are allotted each session to the consideration of estimates and a Liaison Committee, consisting of the chairmen of most of the select committees, determine which estimates are to be considered and the amount of time to be allocated to each. Should the House adopt a select committee report on the estimates, the committee's recommendations would become an order of the House. However, it is important to emphasise that while a proposal to reduce an estimate is in order, it is out of order to propose an increase.

The ancient right of relating grievances to the granting of supply still survives in certain procedures designed to allow additional scope to the opposition and private members. Nineteen days are provided on which the Leader of the Opposition selects the matters to be discussed. These days replace the former 'supply days' which were nominally related to the estimates. They are now simply called 'opposition days', thus formalising a practice which had been of long standing. Private members are provided with a special opportunity following the adoption of the bills (called Consolidated Fund or Appropriation Bills) which give legislative effect to the estimates. Under current procedure these bills are not debatable and their adoption is a formality, albeit a very necessary one. However, at the conclusion of the proceedings a debate takes place which can last throughout the night during which private members have the right to raise matters of their choice. This debate formerly took place on the second reading of the bills concerned, when it could be argued that members were actually raising their concerns before the granting of supply. Their opportunities now occur after the granting of supply, but perhaps it would be pedantic to stress this too much!

A further instrument in the parliamentary oversight of finance is the influential Public Accounts Committee which, with the assistance of the Auditor General, examines departmental expenditures to ensure that all public money is spent as Parliament intended. The committee will expose inefficiency, extravagance and waste and draw attention to any departure from the highest standards of morality in financial matters. By convention the committee is chaired by a senior member of the opposition and the permanent heads of government departments are called before it as witnesses. Its reports are sometimes debated in the House, but such is its prestige that its recommendations usually have the force of directives. Excess expenditure will not even be considered by the House unless the committee believes it to be justified.[4]

The British procedure described above has influenced the financial procedure of many Commonwealth Parliaments, although there is great diversity in matters of detail. In the smaller Parliaments of the Commonwealth the system is far less complex, and as they are not subjected to the same time constraints the opportunities for members to express their concerns are less restricted and the estimates can be examined in greater detail. Many Commonwealth Parliaments have retained the two historic committees of the whole House, the Committee of Supply and the Committee of Ways and Means, which once figured prominently in the financial procedure of the British House of Commons. The Committee of Supply is concerned with the study of estimates, the Committee of Ways and Means with taxation proposals.

Among the larger Parliaments, Canadian procedure has much in common with that of Great Britain, although no legislation corresponding to the annual Finance Bill is required as the taxation structure is maintained under permanent legislation. In the Australian House of Representatives the budget statement is delivered and the budget debate takes place at the second reading of the main Appropriation Bill and the debate can continue for several weeks. In the course of the debate amendments can be moved which concentrate upon specific issues and are invariably framed in terms condemnatory of the government. The estimates are considered at the committee stage of the bill, either in committee of the whole House or by a number of specially constituted estimates committees. The ancient principle concerning the raising of grievances has a place in Australian procedure through the designation of certain days as 'grievance days'. On such days the first item of business is a motion 'that grievances be noted' and the opportunity is used by private members to ventilate their concerns. Speeches are limited to ten minutes and the scope of the debate is virtually unlimited.

In India a general debate takes place on the budget but it is not submitted to a vote of the House in its entirety. Voting opportunities occur during the debates on demands for specific grants, on the Appropriation Bill and on the Finance Bill. Motions to reduce grants, known in India as 'cut motions', normally form the subjects of debate on demands for grants. General debates are allowed on Appropriation Bills although they are restricted to matters which have not been raised during the debates on demands for grants. Wide-ranging debate is allowed on Finance Bills, matters relating to general

78

administration, grievances and the financial and monetary policy of the government being all admissible subjects for discussion. An Estimates Committee consisting of 30 members is appointed to conduct a continuing examination of the estimates throughout the financial year.

Most Commonwealth Parliaments have a system of allotted days or other form of timetable to ensure that the government's financial business shall be finalised by certain dates. Although this is a factor which further inhibits the independence of Parliament, it is today virtually indispensable under the parliamentary system if financial and administrative chaos is to be avoided. Most, if not all, Commonwealth Parliaments appoint a Public Accounts Committee on the British pattern, the chairman usually being a member of the opposition.

US Congressional Practice

If the procedures for financial control under the British parliamentary system seem complex, those established under US congressional procedure are even more so. Only an outline will be attempted within the scope of this book.

The slogan 'no taxation without representation' has the same historic significance for Americans as the right to seek redress of grievances before granting supply has for the British. The drafters of the American constitution, with their colonial experiences fresh in the memory, ensured that overall financial power should be vested in Congress. As with Parliament under the British system, only Congress can levy taxes and appropriate the revenues, but unlike the former the executive does not have the exclusive initiative in financial matters. Furthermore, the President's priorities are not necessarily those of Congress, which always has spending plans of its own. It must nevertheless take full account of the executive's budgetary requirements, so that it is to some extent circumscribed by practical necessity.

The presidential budget is prepared in the Office of Budget and Management which co-ordinates the estimates submitted by federal departments and agencies. Since 1974 Congress has had an office of its own called the Congressional Budget Office which, with a strong staff of professionals, provides both Houses with budgetary forecasts and analysis. The presidential budget is submitted to Congress where it will be taken into account by a number of committees all working simultaneously. Since 1974 each House has appointed a Budget Committee, whose function is to examine the President's budget in the overall context of the financial and economic situation. The legislative committees of the two Houses will consider those parts of the budget which relate to their own jurisdictions. At the same time the House Committee on Appropriations will have had referred to it the expenditure proposals contained in the budget, while the accompanying taxation proposals will have been referred to the House Committee on Ways and Means. Both committees divide their work among sub-committees which undertake the detailed scrutiny of the various parts of the budget assigned to them. The sub-committees hold extensive hearings and the end product of their work is a number of bills which are submitted to the two parent committees. Since budgetary legislation originates in the House of Representatives, these bills must complete their passage in the House before they are referred to the Senate.

However, before this stage is reached the two Budget Committees will have held their own hearings, the legislative committees will have reported the levels of spending on their own programmes to the Budget Committees and the Congressional Budget Office will have provided them with a report on national budget priorities. Equipped with all this information the Budget Committees determine expenditure and revenue targets and submit what amounts to a budget of their own to guide Congress in its subsequent decisions. This forms the basis of a global budget resolution, designed to enable Congress to arrive at a better balance between expenditure and taxation policies.

Following the adoption of this resolution, the budgetary legislation will begin to take shape in the House of Representatives. At this point an important distinction must be made between the authorisation and the appropriation of expenditure. Under House rules, funds cannot be appropriated to a purpose which has not been authorised by legislation. The authorisation of expenditure for specific programmes is a function of the legislative committees, which do not have the power of appropriation. The Appropriations Committee is expected to finance programmes as economically as possible, which clearly offers scope for conflict between this committee and the legislative committees. However, bills reported from the Appropriations Committee have an important edge over those reported from legislative committees. They are accorded priority and are not subject to the authority of the Rules Committee. Bills reported from the Ways and Means Committee are similarly privileged.

The Senate receives budgetary measures from the House in the form of ready-drafted bills. It proceeds in much the same way as the House, referring appropriation bills to its Appropriations Committee and taxation measures to its Finance Committee, the equivalent of the House Ways and Means Committee. There are fewer procedural restrictions in the Senate than in the House, and when these bills finally reach the full Senate they are more likely to be subject to amendment. Differences between the Houses are resolved by conference committees formed of members of the two Appropriations Committees or the Senate Finance Committee and the House Ways and Means Committee, as the case may be.

Throughout the process described above, Congress is guided by the targets expressed in the budget resolution referred to earlier. With the approach of the final date for the adoption of the budgetary bills, Congress once again gives consideration to the budget as a whole. This is the stage at which the budget resolution is modified by reconciliation adjustments arising from changed circumstances, which may in turn require adjustments to the programmes legislated by the legislative committees. Prior to 1980 this was effected through the adoption of a second budget resolution. The annual cycle usually concludes with a bill reconciling the levels of expenditure and taxation with the provisions of the modified resolution.

The American budgetary process is also a process of compromise: compromise between congressional targets and the presidential budget, between congressional spending and executive spending, between various committees, and between the Senate and the House. It is a lengthy process and delay gives rise to problems of its own. The system must also take account of expenditures sanctioned by permanent legislation, which cannot be ignored in determining the overall budget, but which do not fall under the umbrella of the annual appropriations cycle.

Budgetary Practice in France and certain other Countries

In most countries the budgetary initiative rests exclusively with the executive and in most Parliaments committees play an important role in the budgetary process. In France, for example, the fundamentals of the process are laid down in the constitution. A number of financial bills, which must conform to the conditions of an organic law, are introduced annually to determine revenues and expenditures for the fiscal year. The preparation and co-ordination of these bills are the responsibility of the Minister of Finance and they are approved by the Council of Ministers prior to their introduction in the National Assembly, the first step in the parliamentary process. A time-tabling provision in the constitution enables the government to expedite the passage of its budget if necessary. No member of either House is competent to propose amendments which seek to reduce revenues or create or increase a charge on the public.

Financial measures are referred to the Finance Commission of the Assembly[5] for preliminary examination. Every other commission may nominate one or more of its members to participate in an advisory capacity in the work of the Finance Commission, their participation being limited to that part of the budget relative to the area of jurisdiction of the commission concerned. The other commissions may call upon the special rapporteur of the Finance Commission to attend their meetings for the purpose of explaining the provisions of the budget as it applies to them. He may offer advice and must refer to the observations made by members of the other commissions in his reports to the Finance Commission. These reports are made available to the Finance Commission before it begins its examination of each specific part of the budget. All documents required by the commission to enable it to undertake proper scrutiny of the finances of government departments and national enterprises must be furnished to the special rapporteur.

Debate in the Assembly conforms to the standard legislative procedure, the report of the Finance Commission being of crucial importance in influencing the course of the debate. The co-operation of the Finance Commission is a virtual necessity to any Finance Minister anxious to secure a smooth passage for his budget. A general discussion takes place, as in the case of any other bill, followed by a clause-by-clause consideration of the measure when amendments can be proposed. Various restrictions apply to the moving of amendments, and only those called for or agreed to by the government or the Finance Commission have much chance of acceptance. As in the case of any other bill, a second debate on a financial measure may be called for before the vote on the final text. Although any member may call for a second debate, only the government or the commission concerned (in the case of a financial measure, the Finance Commission) may do so as of right. The bill or the parts of the bill concerned are returned to the commission and become the object of a further report prior to the debate, which concentrates only on any new amendments proposed. Once adopted a financial measure is referred to the Senate where it is examined by the Senate Finance Commission and passes through a similar legislative process.

In Italy, where the two Houses of Parliament have equal powers, budget bills are introduced in each House alternately. Each House has a Budget Committee to which the bills are referred. Other committees with specific areas of jurisdiction study those parts of the budget which affect their particular sectors and provide their advice and observations to the Budget Committee. The Budget Committee presents a report to the House which sets the stage for a plenary debate. In Denmark, Finland and Iceland, the detailed examination of the budget is the responsibility of a single Finance Committee, with the result that this committee tends to be overloaded. In Norway and Sweden the various parts of the budget are distributed among specialist committees, a system which has the double advantage of distributing the work-load more equitably and utilising a wider range of expertise.

In Peru the budgetary process is unusual in that it involves joint sittings of both Houses. The budget is considered by Congress as a whole and given preliminary study by a joint committee. Budgetary legislation differs from other legislation in that it is not considered and adopted separately by both Houses. The passage of the budget is subject to a time-table and the system undoubtedly serves to expedite the process. In Guatemala the budget is presented to Congress and immediately referred to the Finance Committee which can hold public hearings and summon ministers before it. It can also hear representations from other committees concerning those parts of the budget which affect the particular ministries they oversee.

The Budgetary Process in the Soviet Union

In the socialist states the budgetary process takes place within the framework of a planned centralised economy. The revised constitution of the Soviet Union provides that the Supreme Soviet, among its responsibilities, shall carry out legislative regulation of relations of ownership, management of the national economy, social and cultural development, the budget and financial system, work remuneration and price formation, the protection of the environment and use of natural resources. The approval of the state plans for economic and social development, of the budget of the USSR and of reports on their execution are among the exclusive prerogatives of the Supreme Soviet, subject under the revised constitution to the overall authority of the Congress of People's Deputies. The preparation of the budget and the annual plan for economic and social development are the responsibility of the Council of Ministers. Both Houses of the Supreme Soviet appoint a number of standing commissions including a Budget and Planning Commission. The two Budget and Planning Commissions are those mainly concerned with the consideration of the plan and the budget, although other commissions may also be involved. They consider the materials provided, hear statements by representatives of government departments and also have access to the reports of consultants and experts. Proposals submitted by the commissions are taken into account by the government before the plan and the budget are considered by the two Houses of the Supreme Soviet at plenary sittings. In the past they were invariably adopted unanimously, the standing commissions having engaged in all the necessary consultations and finalised the detailed work. It remains to be seen how the system will operate under the reforms which, at the time of writing, are in the process of being implemented.

The government pays serious attention to the recommendations of the standing commissions. Consonant with the leadership role accorded to the Communist Party under the Soviet system, many of the members of the commissions have in the past been party members. They provide policy guidance to the commissions with regard to the plan and the budget, which are designed to integrate the many complex and diverse sections of the economy. The commissions concentrate on such goals as improving the efficiency of the national economy, methods of meeting production targets and effecting economies in the use of material and labour resources.

Financial Requirements of the Executive

Methods of financial control vary from country to country, and while the principle of parliamentary sovereignty in budgetary matters is one which is widely held, there is usually a wide gap between the principle and the reality. In the first place, detailed scrutiny of a complex budget poses problems of its own. In the second place, governments must have some assurance of being able to implement their budgetary plans, otherwise a country could fall into financial chaos. Realistic estimation of revenue and expenditure is governed by economic conditions, and any radical alteration of executive proposals could destabilise the entire economy. The priorities of the executive in budgetary matters would therefore seem to be inescapable under any system of government, even in the United States where Congress, potent though its financial powers unquestionably are, cannot ignore the indispensable needs of government.

Methods of Calling the Executive to Account

Parliamentary Control of the Executive

Oversight of the executive is a function of all Parliaments, regardless of the system of government. The effectiveness of the control depends on the extent of Parliament's power in relation to the executive and this is a variable factor. In countries where the executive is directly responsible to Parliament, the latter can bring about the fall of a government by carrying a vote of want of confidence. If the Parliament concerned is bicameral, this power is usually vested exclusively in the popularly elected lower House. In countries where the executive does not look to the legislature to sustain it in office, there are nevertheless methods of calling the executive to account. The US Congress makes extensive use of its committee system for this purpose. In the socialist countries governments report regularly on their activities to the representative assemblies which in most cases have the constitutional powers of appointment, dismissal and recall. In practice these powers are entrusted to the Presidium or equivalent body which provides parliamentary leadership in much the same way that the Communist Party provides political leadership. Ministers are accountable to Parliament in some of the one-party states of Africa, and governments could find themselves facing votes of confidence in certain of them, including Kenya and Zimbabwe. In others, such as Côte d'Ivoire and Senegal, ministers are responsible only to the President of the Republic, although procedures exist which enable Parliament to question the actions of the executive. In most one-party states it is highly unlikely that the executive will be brought down by parliamentary action.

The Issue of 'Confidence'

Most countries which have inherited the British parliamentary system observe the principle of collective cabinet responsibility. The government collectively and ministers individually are answerable to Parliament and a minister unable to accept a particular policy would be obliged to resign.Cabinet solidarity means that an attack on one minister is an attack on the government as a whole. However, in the case of a personal failure on the part of a minister, that minister may resign or be forced to resign and thereby save the government. On major tests of confidence the cabinet stands together. British conventions and precedents are such that a government enjoys a certain flexibility in determining what constitutes an issue of confidence. Some issues leave no room for doubt. The budget is always a major test of confidence, since it underlies the entire range of government policies, and no government denied its budget could possibly carry on. The debate on the speech of the head of state outlining the government's legislative programme at the beginning of a session provides another major test. Amendments to the main motion are usually framed in terms highly critical of the government, and an adverse vote on any such amendment would constitute an expression of want of confidence. Similarly an adverse vote on a motion expressing lack of confidence in specific terms could only be interpreted in one way.

There are other circumstances, however, in which a government might not necessarily feel obliged to resign in the event of a defeat. For example, if a government bill were defeated, it would be up to the government to decide whether the measure was of sufficient significance to constitute a confidence issue, or whether it could accept the loss of the bill and simply carry on. A great deal is likely to depend on the size of the government's majority. A government in a minority situation will be more likely to sustain defeats without considering it necessary to resign than a government with a substantial majority which finds itself deserted by an appreciable number of its own supporters. It is a common misconception that a government under the British system is obliged to resign should it sustain a defeat, regardless of the circumstances. Since it helps to keep their followers in line, governments have little interest in discrediting this myth. The right of the Prime Minister to request a dissolution of Parliament is a very potent one, as it enables him or her in most situations to call for an election at a time the government deems to be favourable for itself. Thus, the right to decide whether an issue constitutes one of confidence or not is a significant weapon in the government armoury.

As an illustration, albeit an unusual one, of how the confidence convention can operate under the British system, we would refer to the vote which brought about the fall of the Chamberlain government in 1940. The motion under debate was simply a motion for the adjournment of the House, such a motion as a peg for a wide-ranging debate being a feature of British procedure. The government had a huge majority in the House, but when the vote was taken a significant number of government supporters either voted against the government or abstained. The government won the vote, but having been deserted by so many of its normal supporters, the Prime Minister decided he had lost the confidence of the House and resigned. Canadian precedents provide another interesting example. In 1968 the government, being in a minority situation, was defeated on the third reading of a budget bill, a classic test of confidence if there ever was one. Instead of resigning, the Prime Minister, Lester Pearson, introduced a motion declaring that the vote did not constitute an expression of want of confidence in the government. The motion was carried with the support of a minor party and the government was saved.

There are many countries, including Commonwealth countries, where the conditions governing confidence motions are less flexible than those described above. In India's *Lok Sabha*, for example, a motion of non-confidence in the government or individual ministers requires the support of not less than fifty members, and if this is obtained the Speaker allots the time for the debate. In France the procedure of the non-confidence motion can be used by the government to serve its own purposes. Under the rules of the National Assembly, the latter may call the government to account by means of a motion of censure provided it is signed by at least one-tenth of the membership. To be adopted, a majority of the total membership – not

86

simply the members present – must vote in its favour, and if defeated no similar motion may be proposed on the initiative of members of the Assembly in the course of the same session. However, in the case of a bill to which the government attaches a particular importance, the Prime Minister can demand a vote on the text, and the bill is considered adopted unless a motion of censure is proposed within 24 hours, such motion being subject to the sponsorship and voting conditions described above. There is no limit to the number of times the government may have recourse to this procedure in the course of a session. In Italy a government once formed must seek a vote of confidence in both Houses of Parliament, which must approve both the composition of the ministry and its programme. Because of the multiplicity of parties in Italy governments depend on the formation of coalitions, which tend to be fragile. A government can face a motion of censure in either House, but a distinction is made between such a motion and an adverse vote on a specific issue. Only the former can lead to the fall of the government and it is subject to a number of conditions, including the sponsorship of at least one-tenth of the membership of the House in which it is introduced.

In West Germany the procedure relating to confidence motions is founded in the Basic Law or constitution, as in France and Italy. A motion expressing lack of confidence in the Federal Chancellor may be introduced in the *Bundestag* provided it is signed by one quarter of the members of the *Bundestag* and proposes a successor by name for election by the *Bundestag*. The Chancellor, for his part, may seek a vote of confidence in the *Bundestag*, and if he fails to obtain it a successor may be elected within 21 days on the motion of one quarter of the members. This system provides an important protection for the government, which would remain in office in the event of failure to name a successor. In the Netherlands non-confidence and censure motions can be introduced in either Chamber as in Italy, and the government can request the dissolution of one of the Houses independently of the other. In the Scandinavian countries, as in Great Britain, governments have a certain flexibility in determining what constitutes a confidence issue. In Sweden, thanks to the protection of the constitution, a government can suffer regular defeats without being obliged to resign unless the issue is declared to be one of confidence. In Finland, however, where the President of the Republic has strong powers, there have been instances of governments being dismissed even though no motion of censure or non-confidence has been passed against them. Other countries where governments can be called upon to face such motions include Austria, Belgium, Greece, Israel, Japan, Jordan, Liechtenstein, Luxembourg, Portugal, Spain and Thailand. In Ireland the practice is similar to that of Great Britain and certain other Commonwealth countries. Among socialist countries whose Parliaments make provision for a non-confidence procedure are Czechoslovakia and Yugoslavia. In Tunisia, a one-party state, a motion of censure may be initiated by one-third of the members and requires a two-thirds majority in order to be adopted. In Peru the Chamber of Deputies must be dissolved if three votes of censure in succession are adopted against the Council of Ministers. The Senate cannot be dissolved until it has run its full term. Under the Peruvian system of government the executive has a wide discretion, including delegated powers to legislate independently of Congress, and the pressures which Congress can bring to bear upon the government are necessarily limited.

Questions and Interpellations

Many Parliaments make provision for a question period, which in some cases takes place on a daily basis, and this provides an important means of calling the government and individual ministers to account. A related procedure, known as interpellation, is an important element in the practice of some Parliaments, since this can give rise to a debate, and in some cases lead to a vote on a confidence issue. This is the case in the French National Assembly where the rules require that a motion of censure signed by at least one-tenth of the members must attach to an interpellation. The rules of the West German *Bundestag* make provision for major and minor interpellations. If the government declines to reply to a major interpellation, a debate may be demanded by a parliamentary group or five per cent of the membership. The interpellation procedure figures in the Parliaments of most European countries, including some of the socialist states. It is also to be found in some Parliaments elsewhere, including those of Argentina, Brazil, Egypt, Jordan, Peru and Thailand.

The rules of the French National Assembly also provide for oral questions, with or without debate, and for written questions. They are addressed to specific ministers, or to the Prime Minister if they concern the general policy of the government. The Conference of Presidents has a wide discretion in determining which questions should give rise to a debate, and they are authorised to combine questions dealing with similar subjects. Written questions may be transformed into oral questions if the government fails to respond within the prescribed time-frame. If a minister, in the course of a debate on a question, indicates that a statement on the same subject is to be made in the course of the next two days, the debate is interrupted and continued when the statement is made. The rules also provide that the government, quite apart from the provisions relating to questions, may seek to make a statement with or without debate, and if a debate is proposed the Conference of Presidents makes the necessary arrangements. If no debate is proposed the President of the Assembly may permit a single deputy to respond to the government. No vote is permitted in the event of a debate so that such statements involve no test of confidence.

Over the years the increase in the use of written questions has been impressive. Oral questions have not had quite the same success, mainly because they are often dealt with in an almost empty chamber, being of interest only to the deputy asking the question and the minister responding. While the number of oral questions without debate continue to be fairly numerous, oral questions followed by a debate are very infrequent.

As the result of an innovation introduced in 1974, for which no provision is made in the rules, the entire Council of Ministers appears every Wednesday from 2.00 p.m. to 4.00 p.m. before the National Assembly to answer questions from members. Each party is allocated an amount of time proportionate to its strength and the entire proceedings are televised. The Council of Ministers also appears before the Senate once a month on a Thursday to answer questions from Senators, a practice dating from 1982.

In the Austrian Parliament the sittings of both Houses commence with a question period. Members may address brief oral questions to the federal government, at least four days notice of a question being required. Supplementary questions may be asked by the questioner and not more than three other members. Provision is also made for written interpellations and the reply, which may be oral or written, may in certain circumstances give rise to discussion. In the *Nationalrat* topical questions concerning the exercise of the executive power of the federal government may also be subjects of discussion but they do not lead to votes or decisions.

Under the British system of parliamentary questions no debate is permitted, although in some Parliaments matters arising out of the question period may be set down for debate on the adjournment motion at the end of the day. The British system provides for oral and written questions, the former being employed by members wishing to give publicity to an issue, the latter by members seeking information of a more detailed nature in a written reply. In the British House of Commons notice is required of all questions answered orally in the House, but supplementary questions are permitted which provide the essence and excitement of the question period. The conditions governing the question period are quite extensive, the cardinal principle being that ministers will only respond to questions on matters for which they are responsible, although there is no obligation on them to respond at all. It is for the Speaker to ensure compliance with the rules relating to questions, and this is probably one of the most exacting tasks the Chair has to face.

The great majority of Parliaments make provision for oral or written questions to ministers and very often both. In some cases the questioning process can lead to a debate, in others not. The British-style question period is to be found in most Commonwealth Parliaments, usually with significant variations. In the Canadian House of Commons, for example, no notice is required of oral questions and the question period is dominated by the opposition parties. It has become an established convention that opposition members are given precedence in the question period and very few government members are recognised by the Chair. The result has been to turn the question period into a daily session of confrontation, the opposition parties hurling charges at the government and ministers responding in kind. The task of the Canadian Speaker during the question period is particularly difficult. Not only does he have no advance notice of the questions, but many of the traditional guidelines have been honoured in the breach rather than the observance, and it is difficult to insist on a respect for precedents which have long been ignored. Provision is also made for written questions and are usually the vehicle employed by members genuinely seeking information. In the Australian House of Representatives provision is made for questions with and without notice, but there is a more equitable division of opportunities between government and opposition members than in Canada. The Speaker gives alternate recognition to members on both sides of the House.

Although the ostensible purpose of parliamentary questions is to seek information or press for action, the political impact of the question period and the public attention given to it have brought about a change in its character over the years in many Parliaments. There is no doubt that the questioning of ministers is a very effective element in calling the executive to account. A minister who is 'on the spot' may well seek to respond to an embarrassing question with a minimum of information,[6] but dramatic results have sometimes been obtained by probing an issue through the question period over a prolonged period.

The revised constitution of the Soviet Union enshrines the right of a deputy to make inquiries of the Chairman of the Supreme Soviet, the Council of Ministers and the heads of other organs of government, an oral or written reply being required within three days. A deputy may exercise this right during sessions of the Congress of Peoples' Deputies and the Supreme Soviet.

Emergency Debates

Most Parliaments make provision for emergency debates, and since they frequently raise issues on which the government is open to criticism they must be counted among the methods of calling the government to account. Under British practice, one which has been adopted by nearly all the Parliaments of the Commonwealth, an emergency debate takes place on a motion for the adjournment of the House. A request for such a debate is governed by stringent conditions which the Speaker must interpret, and the matter is put to the House only if the Speaker determines that the application meets the requirements of the standing order. If accepted by the Chair, the debate is allowed if it is supported by a minimum number of members, which varies from Parliament to Parliament, but which is invariably a small proportion of the total membership in order to prevent the majority suppressing a legitimate request. The procedure is fairly standard in the majority of Commonwealth Parliaments, although a variation is to be noted in Canada, where the Speaker alone decides, and in India where, under the rules of *Lok Sabha*, the Speaker may allow an emergency debate after consulting the member requesting it and a representative of the government. Under Indian procedure no motion is put to the House and no vote is permitted at the end of the debate.

Oversight by Committees

In the United States, in spite of the separation of powers, congressional oversight of the executive is extensive. Early in each new session of Congress the President delivers his State of the Union address to a joint sitting of both Houses. This is followed shortly afterwards by the submission of the presidential budget and a wide variety of departmental reports on executive activities. These reports are referred to the committees having the appropriate jurisdiction in the areas concerned. Committees of both Houses oversee government departments and agencies and conduct investigations into their activities. They are equipped with the research and support staff necessary to enable them to perform effectively, are empowered to subpoena witnesses, including members of the cabinet, and to require the production of documents. A multiplicity of committees is involved in this oversight function and much of the work is delegated to sub-committees. Among the committees appointed are two, one appointed by each House, charged with a general oversight of government operations. They have a very broad mandate and these committees alone handle a tremendous workload. Congress thus uses its committee system as a formidable network of control over the entire range of executive activity.

Procedures for questioning and requiring information from government exist in the Parliaments of all the socialist states. In the Soviet Union oversight of the activities of government is involved in the investigatory work of the standing commissions. Much of this work concerns observance of the law or the development of new laws. The practical realisation of electors' mandates determines much of their activities and they can investigate any problem or study any operation on their own initiative.

The oversight function of committees is common to most Parliaments and is dealt with in greater detail in the next chapter.

Ombudsmen

In some countries another element in the machinery of administrative control is the institution known as the Ombudsman, which originated in Sweden, as far back as 1809, and has been adopted in many jurisdictions. The office is to be found at various levels of government in widely dispersed countries, but it is at the national level that we are concerned with it in this study. The function of the Ombudsman is to investigate the complaints of citizens who claim to have suffered unjust or arbitrary treatment at the hands of public officials. He or she is an officer appointed by the legislature, reports to the legislature and acts independently of executive control. The powers and functions of the Ombudsmen in the countries where the office exists reveal significant variations beyond the scope of this work. Sweden has the most sophisticated system, there being no less than four Ombudsmen of whom one is the Chief Ombudsman and Administrative Director. They share a common office and staff, but each is allocated a defined field of responsibility and they decide their own cases independently. The Chief Ombudsman is responsible for taxation and the execution of judgements, a second covers the courts, police and prisons, a third handles social welfare and education and a fourth the armed forces and all other matters. Between them they cover all agencies and levels of government.

The first countries to follow Sweden's example were Denmark, Finland, New Zealand and Norway. Great Britain appointed a Parliamentary Commissioner for Administration, as the office is styled there, in 1967. However, he may pursue an investigation only on the initiative of a Member of Parliament and a complainant cannot approach him directly. He makes annual reports to Parliament and special reports as required and they are examined by a select committee which deals exclusively with the affairs of the Parliamentary Commissioner. In France the office of *Médiateur* has much in common with the British office and, like the Parliamentary Commissioner, can only be approached through Members of Parliament.

Limiting Debate

In some countries the demands on parliamentary time are very heavy, and membership of Parliament can be a full-time job. In others, Parliament sits during only a short period of the year, and in very small Parliaments all members who wish to participate in a debate can usually do so. In many Parliaments the rules make provision for time limits on speeches and debates. Devices such as closure, which can take various forms, and allocation of time procedures also exist as methods of expediting business. Procedures for limiting debate are sometimes regarded as oppressive of the minority and an obstacle to the proper scrutiny of government measures. However, there is no doubt that unlimited filibustering, if permitted, could bring government to a standstill. The view which is taken of restrictive devices will clearly depend on one's place in the political spectrum. The 'determined opposition' of one group can easily be seen as 'irresponsible obstruction' by another.

In the British House of Commons there are no time limits on speeches and specific limits on the length of debates are only provided for in certain circumstances (e.g., emergency debates are limited to three hours). Nevertheless, a sophisticated system of organising business through negotiation between the government and opposition whips ensures a planned time-table. One result is that the debate on the second reading of a bill seldom exceeds one day. In cases where agreement proves impossible, the government can have recourse to allocation of time motions. The standing orders also provide for the closure, although the Speaker is empowered to refuse it if he believes it to be unfairly claimed. In the Canadian House of Commons, although there are time limits on speeches, debate on the second reading of a bill can extend over several weeks. Much is nevertheless accomplished by inter-party agreement, and the standing orders provide for allocation of time and closure, the latter being less draconian in its operation than in some jurisdictions since, if adopted, debate can continue for several hours before being curtailed. In the Australian House of Representatives the standing orders are designed to favour the government and strict time limits are imposed on both speeches and debates. If closure is carried, debate is curtailed immediately and the Speaker does not have the discretion to refuse it as in Britain.

In the US House of Representatives restrictive devices are many, although different considerations determine how the adversaries are ranged on the floor of the House. Speeches are subject to variable time limits, and procedures for bringing debate to a conclusion include the 'previous question', which is equivalent to closure, and the suspension of the rules on specified days for the purpose of expediting a bill, the latter requiring the permission of the Speaker. Senate procedure is far more relaxed. There is little in the way of restrictive devices and business is organised to a great extent on the basis of unanimous consent. The rules of the French National Assembly make provision for the closure, which can be moved by any member or applied at the discretion of the President, but cannot be invoked if the Conference of Presidents has already organised a debate of a fixed duration. In the West German *Bundestag* a closure motion may be moved by a parliamentary group or five per cent of the membership, but may only be put to the vote if each parliamentary group has had the floor at least once, a condition which in certain circumstances also applies under the French procedure.

Methods of Voting

Methods of voting vary from Parliament to Parliament, a voice vote usually being sufficient where a recorded vote is not required. Recorded votes can take place by roll-call, show of hands, standing in one's place, physical division into lobbies or electronic voting machines, and in some Parliaments more than one method can be used. Some Parliaments also make provision for secret ballots. In Thailand's National Assembly a variety of voting methods are permissible, including secret voting. Electronic voting is one of the options available in the House of Representatives but not the Senate. In the British Parliament members separate into two lobbies when a division is called. In the Canadian Parliament members rise one by one in their places and their names are called in turn by a Clerk-at-the-Table, who must first commit the names of all the members to memory. Electronic voting is used in *Lok Sabha* of India, the US House of Representatives, the French National Assembly, and in Argentina, Belgium, Brazil, Denmark, Egypt, Finland, Italy, Norway, Spain, Sweden and Yugoslavia, although it is not the exclusive method of voting in all of these Parliaments. In a number of Parliaments a recorded vote follows a voice vote only if demanded by a specified minimum number of members. In the great majority of countries, and in most circumstances, voting takes place in public. A number of countries provide for the election of their presiding officers by secret ballot, and several make provision for secret voting in certain circumstances. In Italy, until recently, a secret ballot could be requested by a group chairman or twenty deputies in the Chamber of Deputies. Secret voting frequently took place in the Italian Parliament, and became a highly controversial political issue. In 1988 it was abolished, except in certain circumstances,[7] in the Chamber of Deputies as part of a programme of parliamentary reform. In the

Senate a secret vote may be requested on any matter by twenty senators. In Austria the normal method of voting in both Houses is by standing up (to signify 'aye') or remaining seated (to indicate 'nay'). However, a secret vote may be demanded by the President or five members of the Federal Council or 25 members of the National Council. Cameroon would seem to be one of the very few countries where secret voting is the norm. In China the Presidium decides whether a vote shall take place in public or in private.

The principle underlying parliamentary procedure is that the minority should have its say and the majority should have its way. A recorded vote enables both to register their positions on an issue which is why they are often demanded even when the outcome is a foregone conclusion. Minorities require protection from what is sometimes termed 'the tyranny of the majority' which is why the procedures of Parliament are designed to prevent the majority riding roughshod over their opponents. Occasionally the minority can outwit the majority by means of superior strategy. A good example of this occurred in the British House of Commons in 1969, when a coalition of right-wing conservatives and left-wing socialists, motivated by totally different reasons, forced the abandonment of a bill to reform the House of Lords. The bill was supported in principle by the majority in the three major parties, but it was effectively killed through the use of skilful procedural tactics. The unforeseen is an ever-present element in the operation of Parliament.

Notes

1   Kenneth Bradshaw and David Pring, *Parliament and Congress*, Quartet Books, revised edition, 1982.
2   See Pierre Avril, *Les Français et leur Parlement*, Casterman, 1972, Chapter XII.
3   In the British House of Commons the term 'standing committee' is used to denote a legislative committee.
4   The effectiveness of the Public Accounts Committee has sometimes been criticised on the ground that it performs a post-mortem function. Perhaps the most appropriate retort was provided by Sidney Webb: 'The fact that post-mortem examination does nothing to keep the patient alive is no proof that the existence of a system of post-mortem examinations does not prevent murders'.
5   *La Commission des finances, de l'économie générale et du plan.*
6   A story attributed to Lloyd George, a former British Prime Minister, relates how that gentleman, while motoring in the mountains of North Wales, lost his way and inquired of a passer-by where he was. The passer-by replied: 'You are in a motor car.' Lloyd George subsequently commented that this was the perfect answer to a parliamentary question, since it was true, it was brief, and it told him absolutely nothing he did not know before.
7   A secret vote may still be requested on certain constitutional issues such as those affecting human rights and freedoms, the organs of the state and the electoral laws. The revision of the rules of the chamber and the appointment of commissions of inquiry may also be subject to a secret vote.

6   Committee Systems

The Varying Nature of Parliamentary Committees

All Parliaments work to a greater or lesser extent through committees, and reference has already been made to the operation of certain committees in the course of the previous chapter. Committees can take many forms and perform a variety of functions. Most Parliaments are likely to make use of different kinds of committees and they vary in size as well as purpose. At one end of the scale is the committee of the whole House which, as the term implies, consists of every member of the House. A committee appointed to undertake a specialised task is likely to be quite small, a good example being the task forces consisting of seven members which the Canadian House of Commons has appointed from time to time to inquire into such matters as the problems of the handicapped and alternative sources of energy. Some committees have very broad mandates, some have very narrow ones. Some are appointed on the basis of subject specialisation. Some have strictly financial responsibilities. Some are appointed to deal with legislation, in particular to give detailed clause-by-clause study to a bill. Some can initiate their own investigations, others require a specific reference from the House which appoints them. Some have an ongoing existence, being appointed for the duration of a Parliament or a session. Others are appointed to perform a single function and cease to exist when their work is done. In bicameral Parliaments provision is frequently made for the appointment of joint committees, both standing and *ad hoc*. The powers of committees vary from Parliament to Parliament. In the United States, for example, congressional committees have considerable scope for independent action. Under the British parliamentary system, committees, while equipped with the powers necessary to do their work, are limited to making reports and recommendations to the House.

    Except in the case of very small Parliaments, a legislative chamber in its plenary form is usually too big to deal efficiently with matters of detail or to undertake inquiries. In the smaller Parliaments of the Commonwealth, such as those of St. Lucia in the Caribbean or Nauru in the Pacific, the detailed consideration of bills and financial business takes place in committee of the whole House, but even these small Parliaments appoint smaller committees for other purposes. The committee of the whole House derives from the 'grand' or 'general' committee which developed in the English House of Commons during the reigns of James I and Charles I. Such committees, where discussion could be more informal and less restricted, became forums for debating weighty matters of church and state and the House would resolve that all members who attended would have voices. The committee of the whole came to be an essential feature of House of Commons practice. Prior to 1882 all bills were referred to committees of the whole House for clause-by-clause consideration, and until 1966 a vast range of financial business was debated in detail in committees of the whole. The Committees of Supply and Ways and Means had traditionally dealt with the estimates of expenditure and taxation proposals and a bill involving expenditure was preceded by a financial resolution adopted in committee of the whole. The financial procedure of the House was radically reformed in 1966, and this change, coupled with the fact that the great majority of bills are now referred to legislative committees (misleadingly called standing committees), has greatly reduced the significance of the committee of the whole in British practice. It is used more frequently for the discussion of bills in the House of Lords, but since 1968 Public Bill Committees, consisting of twelve or fourteen peers, have also been appointed for the consideration of bills after second reading. The committee of the whole House continues to exist in most Commonwealth Parliaments, India being a notable exception.

Most Parliaments today deal with a vast range of public affairs and the development of committees has reflected this ever-increasing work-load. It is frequently necessary to examine witnesses when pursuing an investigation, and this can more conveniently be undertaken by a small committee than by the House as a whole. The power to summon witnesses, including the power to subpoena, is therefore frequently delegated to committees, together with the power to call for documents and records, and the authority to travel and engage additional staff, whenever these powers are required to enable a committee to fulfil its mandate.

Parliamentary Committees in Great Britain and other Commonwealth Countries

An outline of the committee system of the British House of Commons will give an indication of the great diversity of committees which can operate under a single parliamentary umbrella. The important part played by committees in the legislative process has already been mentioned. The standing committees referred to above are appointed as required to deal with specific bills. They range in size from sixteen to fifty members, who are nominated by a committee called the Committee of Selection, having regard to their qualifications in relation to the bill under consideration and the composition of the House. Although styled standing committees, they have no continuing membership and are distinguished only by a letter of the alphabet. There is no limit to the number which may be appointed at any one time. Certain other committees of a different character are also called standing committees. These include the Scottish Grand Committee, the Welsh Grand Committee, the Northern Ireland Committee and the Standing Committee on Regional Affairs which deals with matters relating to the regions of England. These committees have broader mandates than those concerned exclusively with the detailed study of bills. Occasionally a bill is referred for consideration in principle to a Second Reading Committee, which is also categorised as a standing committee, and such a bill may also be referred subsequently to a standing committee at its report stage. Standing committees are also appointed to consider European Community documents and statutory instruments (regulations made under the authority of an Act of Parliament). The chairmen of standing committees are drawn from the Chairmen's Panel, which includes both government and opposition members. They preside impartially and are equipped with many of the powers of the Speaker in the House.

In a different category of committees are those which are styled select committees. Fourteen of these are related to government departments, and they are empowered to examine the expenditure, administration and policy of the particular departments assigned to them. They consist of nine, eleven or thirteen members and can initiate their own inquiries. Other select committees include the Committee of Public Accounts, to which reference has already been made, and the Committee of Privileges, which considers any matter concerning the rights and immunities of the House and its members which may be referred to it. They are both very senior committees with a long historic tradition behind them. The House of Commons Services Committee deals with accommodation, the library, catering and other internal services and works through a series of sub-committees. Select committees of more recent origin include those on the Parliamentary Commissioner for Administration, European Legislation, Sound Broadcasting and Members' Interests. A Liaison Committee, consisting of the chairmen of most of the select committees, co-ordinates the work of select committees, oversees foreign travel and seeks to prevent duplication of work. It also recommends how time should be allocated to the estimates on days when they are considered on the floor of the House. The Liaison Committee is the largest of the select committees, consisting of 23 members, and the Select Committee on Sound Broadcasting is the smallest, consisting of six. It is, of course, open to the House to appoint any other select committee on an *ad hoc* basis as it sees fit.

There are sixteen sessional committees in the House of Lords, some of them having highly specialised functions such as those dealing with private legislation and matters relating to the appellate jurisdiction of the House. Some of them, including the Committee for Privileges, the Committee of Selection, the Committee on Sound Broadcasting, the House of Lords Offices Committee and the European Communities Committee, have their counterparts in the House of Commons. The House of Lords also appoints a Procedure Committee on a sessional basis and a Science and Technology Committee. An important committee appointed jointly by the two Houses is the Joint Committee on Statutory Instruments whose function is to oversee the regulation-making power of the executive with a view to ensuring that the latter does not exceed the authority conferred on it by statute. Unlike a House of Commons standing committee to which a statutory instrument is referred, the Joint Committee is not concerned with matters of policy.

The committee system of Canada's Parliament has much in common with that of Great Britain. Both the Senate and the House of Commons make use of the committee of the whole House, but in the latter it is mainly used to expedite the passage of a bill with the agreement of all parties. Most bills in the House of Commons are referred to legislative committees similar to the standing committees of the British House of Commons. They consist of a maximum of 30 members and are chaired by members from a similar panel of chairmen. There are 19 standing committees, other than joint committees, which correspond in many ways to the British select committees. Most of them relate to government departments and can initiate their own inquiries. They range in size from seven to fifteen members. Legislative committees, unlike their British counterparts, share with standing committees the right to call witnesses. The Senate appoints eleven standing committees, other than joint committees, most of them consisting of twelve members and concerned with areas of subject specialisation. Both Houses also appoint special committees to undertake specific investigations, and in recent years the Senate has launched a number of in-depth studies of issues of great social and economic significance through the appointment of special committees. The House of Commons appoints a Liaison Committee consisting of the chairmen of all the standing committees, whose function is to apportion the funds required to meet the expenses of committee activities. There are two important standing joint committees, one of which monitors the policy and programmes relating to the two official languages, the other being charged with the scrutiny of delegated legislation and having terms of reference similar to those of its British counterpart.

The committee system of the Australian Parliament reveals both differences and similarities in respect of British and Canadian practice. Both the Senate and the House of Representatives use the committee of the whole House for the consideration of bills, and in the latter a legislation committee is sometimes appointed by sessional order. Fewer committees are provided for by standing order than in Britain or Canada, but it is open to either House to appoint a committee either on a sessional or *ad hoc* basis by resolution. An important feature of the Senate committee system is the group of Estimates Committees and Legislative and General Purpose Standing Committees first established in 1970. The former are able to carry out a more probing examination of the operations of government departments than was previously possible. The latter, of which there are now eight provided for by standing order, have broad subject mandates and are able to initiate their own inquiries. All these committees are small and membership is equally divided between government and opposition. Another committee appointed by the Senate is the Regulations and Ordinances Committee, which performs the same functions as the comparable joint committees of the British and Canadian Parliaments.

The committee system of the House of Representatives underwent important changes in 1987, and for the first time a structure was put in place which enables the House to monitor the work of all government departments. Previously, committees were regularly appointed by resolution of the House, some having wide mandates and an ongoing existence in which case they were called standing committees, others having a more limited existence in which case they were called select committees. Under the new system, eight general purpose standing committees, together with a Joint Committee on Foreign Affairs, Defence and Trade having extended functions, have been established. The mandates of these committees ensure that every department of government and statutory authority is subject to parliamentary oversight. Most of these standing committees consist of twelve members, the ratio between government and

100

opposition being seven to five. The Joint Committee on Foreign Affairs, Defence and Trade consists of thirty members, eleven being senators and nineteen members of the House. Membership of the standing committees may be supplemented by up to three additional members for a particular inquiry. Unlike the subject-oriented committees of the British and Canadian Parliaments, their counterparts in the Australian House of Representatives cannot initiate their own inquiries. They require a reference from the House or the appropriate minister, but should a committee wish to pursue a particular inquiry a request to the minister concerned that the matter be referred to it is usually successful.

There are three joint committees established by statute, the Parliamentary Standing Committee on Public Works, the Joint Committee on the Broadcasting of Parliamentary Proceedings and the Joint Committee of Public Accounts.

In the Indian Parliament there are two basic categories of committees, *ad hoc* committees and standing committees. Most of the *ad hoc* committees are select and joint committees which consider bills. Many of the standing committees appointed by *Lok Sabha* are 'watchdog' committees, including the Public Accounts Committee, the Committee on Public Undertakings, the Estimates Committee, the Committee on Subordinate Legislation and the Committee on Government Assurances. They all consist of 15 members, except the Estimates Committee which consists of thirty, and the first two have in addition seven members of *Rajya Sabha* associated with their work. The Committee on Government Assurances is of particular interest, its mandate being to scrutinise the assurances given from time to time by ministers and report on the extent to which they have been implemented. Among other committees appointed by *Lok Sabha* is the Business Advisory Committee which is chaired by the Speaker and includes representatives of most parliamentary groups. It recommends the time to be allotted to the various items of government business and can also propose particular subjects for discussion.

Among the committees appointed in the National Assembly of Zambia are nine sessional committees, all being nominated by the Speaker except the Public Accounts Committee which is elected by the House. One of these committees is a Committee on Government Assurances, having a similar mandate to its Indian counterpart. There are many similarities among committees throughout the Parliaments of the Commonwealth. Most commonly found are those dealing with such matters as estimates, public accounts, privileges, procedure, and the oversight of delegated legislation.

The French System

The French parliamentary committee system differs markedly from the British and those which derive from the British practice. Although British-style parliamentary committees play an important role in the legislative process and the control of the executive, it is a subordinate one. By contrast, French parliamentary committees are the essential instruments in these processes and a considerable measure of power is delegated to them. There are two categories, standing commissions and special commissions, the former being basic to the French parliamentary structure. Under the Fourth Republic there was no limit to the number of standing commissions which could be appointed, and they virtually controlled the legislative programme since cabinets seldom survived long enough to provide legislative stability. The constitution of the Fifth Republic placed certain limits on the sovereignty of Parliament. Certain spheres of legislative action are reserved to the executive, and the number of standing commissions which can be appointed by either House is limited to six. Their powers have been reduced as an inevitable consequence of the reduction in the power of Parliament itself, yet they have assumed a new importance since upon them falls the responsibility of protecting the authority of Parliament from further erosion.

The standing commissions have very large memberships and their mandates are designed to prevent them being too specialised. In the National Assembly two of them may consist of up to one quarter of the total membership of the House (about 120 members) and the other four of up to one eighth (about 60). Of the two largest, one deals with cultural, family and social affairs, the other with production and exchange (covering a wide range of subjects including agriculture, transport, energy and industry). The others deal respectively with foreign affairs; defence and the armed forces; finance, economic affairs and planning; and constitutional law, legislation and the general administration of the Republic. The standing commissions of the Senate range in size from 40 to 78 members and, although not the exact counterparts of those of the National Assembly, they cover the same range of responsibilities. In neither House may a member belong to more than one standing commission.

Special commissions may be appointed on the initiative of the government or the House concerned, their size being limited to 31 in the Assembly and 24 in the Senate. No specific criterion governs their appointment. They may be set up to deal with legislation or other matters overlapping the mandates of two or more standing commissions, to deal with issues which are narrow in scope, or any other matter thought to be more appropriate for a special commission.

Since special commissions tend to be more specialised than standing commissions, their members usually have a particular interest in the matter before them. In the view of some commentators, special commissions offer better opportunities for meaningful scrutiny of government measures. In the National Assembly no special commission may include more than fifteen members of any one standing commission. Provision exists in both Houses for the appointment of commissions of inquiry or control, usually for the purpose of examining the administration of a government department. Joint commissions consisting of seven members from each House are appointed to discuss matters of disagreement between the Senate and the National Assembly.

All commissions are composed on a proportional basis so as to reflect the party standings in the House concerned. Both standing commissions and special commissions elect a bureau or directing authority. In the National Assembly a standing commission elects at least three vice-presidents and three secretaries in addition to its president, and the bureau of a special commission consists of a president, two vice-presidents and two secretaries. A Senate standing commission elects a president, four vice-presidents and four secretaries, while a special commission may itself decide the composition of its bureau. In both Houses the *rapporteur général* of the Finance Commission is a member of that commission's bureau. The Finance Commission is the dominant commission in both Houses, since it has the right to consider any bill which has financial implications. Its authority thus overlaps in quite a fundamental way that of all the other commissions.

Occasionally a bill or other matter which overlaps the mandates of two standing commissions may be considered by both. In such a case the commission most directly concerned becomes *la commission saisie au fond*, and the other, having requested permission to consider the matter in an advisory capacity, becomes *la commission saisie pour avis*. The rapporteur of each commission is entitled to attend the meetings of the other in a consultative capacity.

The rapporteur of a commission, and in particular the *rapporteur-général* of the Finance Commission in each House, plays a crucial role in the legislative process. It is the rapporteur who first studies and analyses the legislation. He or she consults with interested parties, suggests the witnesses whom the commission should hear, gives advice on any amendments proposed, and prepares a comparative report on the text of the bill in relation to any legislation already in force and any amendments proposed.

The System in other Western European Countries

The West German *Bundestag* appoints subject-oriented standing committees for the preparation of its legislative deliberations and special committees to study specific questions. It may also set up study commissions to deal with wide-ranging and significant issues, and the appointment of a study commission is obligatory if a motion for the purpose is proposed by one quarter of the total membership of the *Bundestag*. A number of committees are provided for under the Basic Law (constitution). These include committees of investigation, which the *Bundestag* is obliged to appoint if demanded by one quarter of the membership, the Committee for the Scrutiny of Elections, the Committee on Foreign Affairs, the Committee on Defence and the Petitions Committee which deals with requests and complaints from the public. Three other committees are appointed under the Basic Law. The Committee for the Election of Judges consists of the Ministers of Justice of each *Land* and an equal number of members elected by the *Bundestag*. The Committee of Delegates elects the members of the Federal Constitutional Court and consists of an equal number of members of the *Bundestag* and the *Bundesrat*. The Mediation Committee, which also consists of an equal number of members of the *Bundestag* and the *Bundesrat*, is convoked to consider any bill on which the two Houses have failed to agree. The committee may propose amendments to such a bill, and while in most cases a bill can be adopted over the objections of the *Bundesrat*, the Mediation Committee has been very successful in resolving conflicts. Like the *Bundestag*, the *Bundesrat* also appoints subject-oriented committees which correspond broadly with the responsibilities of government departments. Each *Land* is represented on every committee and each has one vote.

The rules of the Italian Chamber of Deputies provide for three special committees concerned respectively with procedure, elections and members' immunities; and 14 subject-oriented standing committees.

The Committee on Procedure consists of the President of the Chamber of Deputies as chairman and ten members appointed by him. The committee considers any proposals concerning the rules and advises on their interpretation. It also resolves conflicts of jurisdiction among the standing committees. It recommends to the House any amendments to the rules which it deems necessary, such amendments requiring an absolute majority of the members in order to be adopted. The Election Committee consists of 30 members appointed by the President of the Chamber and is concerned with the regularity of election procedures, the conditions of the admission of members and cases of ineligibility and incompatibility. Members

104

appointed to this committee may neither refuse to be nominated nor resign. The committee once formed elects a chairman, two vice-chairmen and three secretaries. The Committee for Authorisations deals with any request involving the waiving of a member's immunity. It consists of 21 members appointed by the President of the Chamber and recommends for or against authorisation to proceed against a member, either by way of criminal prosecution, issuing of a search warrant, or any other procedure affecting a member's personal liberty. The committee will hear any member involved in such a case before reaching a decision. It elects a chairman, two vice-chairmen and three secretaries. Care is taken to ensure that the members appointed to these three committees are representatives of the parliamentary groups in proportion to their strength in the House.

The rules of the House do not specify the size of the standing committees, but each parliamentary group appoints its representatives to each committee according to the number assigned to it. The President of the Chamber appoints additional members to improve the representative balance and ensure that the smaller parliamentary groups are accorded places on some committees. No member may be appointed to more than one standing committee. Each standing committee elects a chairman, two vice-chairmen and two secretaries. The standing committees have various functions. They investigate any matters referred to them and report their recommendations to the House. They act both as advisory bodies and legislative bodies. In their legislative capacity they debate and approve bills falling within their area of subject responsibility and they can also be called upon to draft bills. They consider and discuss government communications and are involved in policy-making, oversight of the executive and the provision of information. The Chamber may at any time appoint *ad hoc* committees having similar functions to the standing committees.

The Senate has a committee structure similar to that of the House, although there are some differences to be noted. There is a Committee on Procedure consisting of the President of the Senate as chairman and ten other senators, an Elections and Parliamentary Immunity Committee consisting of 21 senators and a Library Committee composed of three senators. There are twelve subject-oriented standing committees having functions similar to those of the standing committees of the Chamber of Deputies. In addition the rules provide for a Committee for the European Communities and for the appointment of *ad hoc* committees as required. Provision is also made for joint committees of the two Houses. The two Houses may either separately or jointly set up a Committee of Inquiry, such committees having the same powers as the judiciary.

An interesting procedure common to both Houses is one whereby minor bills may be given final approval by a standing or *ad hoc* committee without the subsequent endorsement of the House concerned. In the Chamber of Deputies a proposal to deal with a bill in this manner may be made by the President, and it can be blocked if either the government or one-tenth of the members object. Otherwise, if there is opposition, one member in favour and one against the proposal may be heard, after which the matter is decided by a show of hands. This procedure is also sometimes adopted for bills of special urgency. In the Senate the President may in his discretion, having informed the Senate, assign minor bills for final approval to a standing or *ad hoc* committee, but the government, one-tenth of the senators or one-fifth of the members of a committee may call for the bill to be returned to the Senate for the final vote.

Both Houses of the Belgian Parliament appoint standing and special committees, the numbers in each case being unspecified. Standing committees of the House of Representatives consist of 23 members, while in the Senate both standing and special committees consist of 22. In the former House the terms of reference and designations of the standing committees are determined by the President of the Chamber following consultations with the leaders of the parliamentary groups. In the Senate this determination is made by the Bureau. Standing and special committees of both Houses deal with, among other things, legislation and budgetary matters. Both Houses also appoint a Petitions Committee, which determines the action to be taken on petitions received from members of the public, and a Naturalisation Committee, which examines individual applications for naturalisation. The House of Representatives appoints a number of other committees dealing with such matters as European questions;[1] social emancipation; conflict of interest; and constitutional revision.

In Switzerland standing and special committees are appointed in both chambers and they are responsible for the initial drafting of all decisions taken by Parliament. The Council of States has nine standing committees, all having their equivalents in the National Council which has a total of eleven. Of particular importance are the Finance Committees, the Control Committees, the Committees for Petitions and Examination of Cantonal Constitutions, and the Foreign Affairs Committees. The Finance Committees examine the budget and accounts of the Confederation and are divided into sub-committees which oversee the financial management of the various departments. A 'finance delegation' consisting of three members of each House maintains constant supervision of the financial management of the country as a whole. The Control Committees review the conduct of business of the Federal Council (cabinet), the Federal

Tribunal and the departments of government and are divided into eight sub-committees corresponding to the federal departments and the Post and Telecommunications Corporation. The Committees for Petitions and Examination of Cantonal Constitutions protect the political rights of the people and the cantons and ensure that the cantonal constitutions do not conflict with the provisions of the Federal Constitution. The Foreign Affairs Committees, in addition to their oversight function relating to foreign policy in general, have a special responsibility concerning international treaties, development aid and federal building projects abroad. In addition to the standing committees appointed by each House, there are three joint standing committees: the Documentation Committee, concerned with internal documentation services; the Pardons Committee, which examines requests for the pardoning of convicted persons; and the Drafting Committee, which re-drafts laws which have been heavily amended.

Subject-oriented standing committees play a crucial part in the legislative process in all the Scandinavian Parliaments which, like committees in many other Parliaments, tend to be overloaded. The burgeoning output of legislation, initiated both by government and members themselves, provides a workload which inevitably results in the consideration of some proposals being postponed or set aside, and the private initiatives of members are the ones which tend to suffer. In all the Scandinavian Parliaments a matter may be referred to a committee at any stage, and committees often meet during parliamentary recesses in order to keep up with their work. In Sweden three important committees are set up under the provisions of the constitution, those on the constitution, finance and taxation. Of particular interest in the Scandinavian region is the 'upper-tier' committee to be found in Finland known as the Grand Committee. It consists of at least 45 members of the *Eduskunta*, provision being made for alternate members. It considers all bills reported from the specialist standing committees and can propose amendments of its own. It is essentially a committee of review and to some extent fulfils the role of an upper House – at least, this was the original intention behind its creation. In common with the other parliamentary committees, it carries a heavy work-load which may be an inhibiting factor in its effectiveness.

The System in Israel

In the *Knesset* of Israel there are ten standing committees, appointed for the duration of a Parliament, nine of which are subject-oriented. The tenth, the House Committee, is of paramount importance because of the decisive role it plays in the overall operation of the

Knesset. It controls the organisation of business and determines the day-to-day agenda. No amendment to the rules of procedure is adopted unless first recommended by the committee. It is involved in the consideration of election appeals and disciplinary action against members. It may initiate legislation concerning the rights, immunities and emoluments of members. It may, in case of disagreement, determine the standing committee to which a bill should be assigned. While most of its decisions, other than those made in terms of powers conferred on it by the rules of the House, require the endorsement of the *Knesset* itself, a recommendation of the House Committee carries very great weight and is unlikely to be reversed.

Most of the work of the other committees is concerned with legislation and the rules of the *Knesset* require that they give precedence to bills. They also have statutory functions. Some laws require that executive regulations and orders must be approved by the appropriate committee. The Finance Committee, which deals with budgetary matters, taxation, banking and currency, has a wide range of responsibilities conferred on it by various statutes. The standing committees are free to consider any matter within their subject areas on their own initiative. They may report the results of any such study directly to the minister concerned. Because of the heavy volume of business handled by the standing committees, much of their work is delegated to sub-committees.

The *Knesset* may also appoint special committees and committees of inquiry. A special committee, usually appointed on the recommendation of the House Committee, is set up only rarely to deal with a very specific or particularly sensitive issue. Most matters are dealt with by the standing committees, and if the subject overlaps the responsibilities of two standing committees, a mixed or joint committee, consisting of an equal number of members of both, may be set up to deal with it. The House Committee determines the composition of the joint committee and also decides which of the standing committee chairmen shall preside over it. Standing committees are not empowered to subpoena witnesses, but when a special inquiry is called for, a committee of inquiry equipped with the necessary powers may be appointed, or alternatively, the appropriate standing committee may be invested with those powers.

Committee chairmanships are allocated by agreement between the parliamentary groups which, as far as possible, are represented on the various committees in proportion to their strengths. The chairmen have considerable powers regarding the calling of meetings and the organisation of committee business. They can even delay the progress of legislation, although it is more difficult than it would be in a US congressional committee to block a bill completely.

The System in Japan

The Japanese constitution provides for the appointment of standing committees in both Houses of the Diet, most of them corresponding with the departments of government. In addition both Houses may appoint special committees to examine specific issues, and some of them are regularly appointed on a sessional basis. The House of Representatives has eighteen standing committees ranging in size from 20 to 50 members, and the House of Councillors has sixteen ranging from ten to 45 members. The responsibilities of sixteen of the standing committees of the House of Representatives correspond exactly to those of their counterparts in the House of Councillors, the former having in addition a Committee on Science and Technology and a Committee on Environment. The four standing committees in both Houses which do not correspond with government departments are those on Budget, Audit, Rules and Administration, and Discipline. Except for members of the government, every Diet member must serve on at least one standing committee. Members of standing committees are appointed by the presiding officers on the recommendation of the parties, each being accorded a number of places proportionate to its strength in the House concerned. Appointment of the chairmen is also entrusted to the presiding officers. Each standing committee has a directorate, the number of directors for each committee being determined by the Committee on Rules and Administration after each election. Directorships are distributed among the parties in proportion to their strengths, and the members appointed become the negotiators and managers of the business of their respective committees. The Committee on Rules and Administration also has the task of fixing the dates of plenary sittings, arranging the order of business, deciding the number and order of speakers and the allocation of time to each, and dealing with the general administration of the House.

In both Houses the Budget Committee is the largest of all the committees. The Budget Committee of the House of Representatives is probably a greater focus of public attention than any other committee. The budget is first presented to the House of Representatives and referred to its Budget Committee where wide-ranging debate takes place. The meetings are usually attended by members of the cabinet, any matter within government responsibility may be raised, and advantage is taken of the occasion to thrash out the controversial issues of the day. The process continues in sub-committees to which are referred the various sections of the budget. The affairs of the nation thus receive exhaustive discussion in the committee and its sub-committees before the budget is reported to the House in its plenary form where further debate will take place.

US Congressional Committees

The extensive powers of US congressional committees have already been indicated in the previous chapter. In most Parliaments, committees operate as component parts of the parent machine. By contrast, US congressional committees operate to a great extent as self-contained entities with a wide measure of independence. Both Houses appoint a range of standing committees of widely varying character, there being at the time of writing 16 in the Senate and 22 in the House of Representatives. The fate of legislation is largely determined by these committees. It is difficult, and sometimes impossible, to overcome the obstacle of a committee which is determined to block the progress of a bill. In practice it is the committees which control the legislative agenda as Congress usually deals only with those bills which have been reported from committees. Congressional committees have, in fact, been described as 'little legislatures', in recognition of the extent to which Congress has surrendered its initiative to its committees. Standing committees are also mandated to oversee the government departments and agencies falling within the scope of their subject responsibilities and their unlimited power of investigation further augments their influence.

The standing committees operate to a great extent through sub-committees, which vary in importance from committee to committee. Committees having more than twenty members are required to establish at least four sub-committees and many of them operate with a large degree of autonomy in their own right. The proliferation of sub-committees has led to literally thousands of meetings of committees and sub-committees taking place during the two-year term of a Congress.

Committee chairmen, and many sub-committee chairmen as well, are powerful figures in the American congressional system, and some senators and congressmen have become nationally renowned through their chairmanship of important committees. Chairmanships, of both committees and subcommittees, belong as of right to the majority party in the House concerned. Chairmen call the meetings, establish the agendas, arrange hearings, control the funds and staff of their committees and give general direction to their activities. A chairman could kill a bill through procedural manipulation, although in the light of recent reforms, he or she would probably require the support of the majority of the committee in order to succeed. A bill suppressed in this way might nevertheless be one supported by the majority of the House as a whole. For this reason, strategic considerations are called for in the allocation of bills to committees. There are intense rivalries and overlapping responsibilities between committees and it is sometimes necessary, in order to ensure a bill's passage, to draft it in such a way as to guarantee its referral to a sympathetic committee. It is the function of the presiding officer in each House to assign bills to the appropriate committee.

At one time chairmen were even more powerful than they are today. Under an unwritten convention known as the seniority rule, the majority party member of longest uninterrupted service on a particular committee automatically became the chairman. Committee chairmen therefore tended to be elderly, conservative senators and congressmen who had long represented states and districts which were electorally safe. It was they who appointed the chairmen of sub-committees. During the 1970's a number of reforms were effected, whereby committee chairmen are now elected by their party caucus and sub-committee chairmen by the party majority on the committee. These changes did not automatically deprive senior members of their chairmanships, but it made them more responsive to their colleagues and opened up some of the more important sub-committee chairmanships to more junior members. Among other reforms, all standing committees were given the power of subpoena, and in the House of Representatives subcommittees were allocated independent budgets and authorised to hire their own staff and arrange their own schedules.

Congress also appoints special committees and joint committees, which usually have investigative rather than legislative functions, some of them being appointed on a continuing basis. A joint committee known as a conference committee is convened whenever it is necessary to resolve a disagreement between the two Houses. The committee of the whole House also features in congressional procedure. In the Senate it is used only for the consideration of treaties. In the House of Representatives it is usually resorted to for the purpose of expediting an item of business.

Systems of some Latin American Countries

The US Congress probably has the distinction of being the Parliament with the greatest number of committees if sub-committees are included. If they are excluded the Congress of Mexico may well be able to claim the record. At the apex of the system in each House of the Mexican Congress is a Great Committee, presided over by the President of the chamber concerned. The Great Committee of the Senate consists of one senator from each state and the federal district; that of the Chamber of Deputies consists of a representative of each regional district and parliamentary group. Each House appoints 52 standing committees, some corresponding with government departments, others having overlapping responsibilities. The Great Committees nominate the members of the standing committees who are then formally elected by the respective Houses. Special committees and joint committees are also appointed, and provision is made for special committees of inquiry which may be appointed in the Senate at the request of one half of the senators and in the Chamber of Deputies at the request of one quarter of the members. The life of the Great Committees and of the standing committees is three years and of a special committee one year. A joint committee and a special committee of inquiry continue until the task or investigation has been completed.

In the Congress of Argentina, as in many other Parliaments, committees are indispensable to the functioning of the system and much of the work of Congress is transacted in its committees. Apart from dealing with virtually all the legislation brought before the Congress,[2] the standing committees of both Houses play a major liaison role between Congress and the public. They maintain contact with pressure groups and representatives of community interests, sound out public opinion on the issues before them, and seek information and advice from a wide range of extra-parliamentary sources. Because of the diversity and complexity of the many issues examined, the number of standing committees appointed is considerable and a sharply defined distribution of work is designed to promote efficiency and the most profitable use of the time available. The Senate appoints 29 standing committees, some of nine members, some of seven. The Chamber of Deputies appoints 28, ranging in size from 15 to 25 members, with the exception of the Committee on Budget and Finance which consists of 31. Both Houses may also appoint special committees and committees of inquiry and provision is also made for joint committees. A joint committee consisting of two senators and three deputies, and chaired by a senator, examines the accounts of the administration. Another kind of committee, known as a committee of control, which may be joint or appointed separately by either House, is the means whereby Congress reviews the actions of the executive. This oversight function, regarded as an implicit power of the Congress since it is nowhere specified in the constitution, has been the subject of debate as to how far the power extends. The appointment of committees of control have thus sometimes given rise to controversy.

In the Congress of Guatemala a committee is appointed to oversee every ministry, the members of each committee being elected annually by Congress as a whole. Provision is also made for the appointment of *ad hoc* committees. An interesting feature of the committee system of the Congress of Peru is the arrangement whereby a joint committee of five senators and ten deputies exercises the powers of the Congress when it is in recess.

Standing commissions have operated in the Soviet Union ever since the Supreme Soviet met for the first time in 1938. At the outset four were formed in each chamber, and they were active throughout the Second World War, assisting the Presidium in the preparation of the necessary measures for regulating the lives of a people fighting a war of survival. After the war the number and activities of the standing commissions broadened considerably, and in 1967 the Supreme Soviet adopted the Statute for Standing Commissions regulating their activities on a more systematic basis. The membership and number of standing commissions are determined by the two chambers, and it has been the practice in the past to appoint parallel commissions charged with the same mandates. Between them they covered the entire range of public affairs, each consisting of 35 members except the Planning and Budget Commissions which had 45.

At the time of writing it is not known whether exactly the same practices will continue. The revised constitution provides that both chambers of the Supreme Soviet will appoint standing commissions from among their own members and other members of the Congress of People's Deputies and that committees of the Supreme Soviet may also be appointed by the two chambers on a parity basis. They will perform legislative work, make a preliminary review of matters coming within the jurisdiction of the Supreme Soviet, promote the implementation of laws and oversee the performance of state bodies and organisations. Commissions of inquiry and audit may also be appointed, together with commissions on any other matter whenever it is deemed necessary. Up to one-fifth of the members of all standing commissions and other committees must be replaced annually. Members of the Presidium and the holders of certain other offices are not eligible to serve on them. Since the standing commissions and other committees perform an oversight function in respect of executive bodies, membership is judged to be incompatible with the holding of government office. The great majority of the 1500 members of the former Supreme Soviet were members of standing commissions, and it may be assumed that most of the members elected to the Supreme Soviet under the new system will also be active on committees.

Members of standing commissions are chosen with regard to their qualifications and experience. Thus, those standing commissions concerned with industry and production include both workers and directors of state enterprises. Those concerned with agriculture include workers on collective farms as well as agricultural experts. The professional and occupational spectrum of Soviet life is reflected in the standing commissions, and their work is ongoing, quite independently of the sessions of the Supreme Soviet.

More than 50% of the membership has been and may continue to be required to form a quorum at a standing committee meeting. Since a majority of the members of the former Supreme Soviet were members of the Communist Party, it followed that a majority of the members of the standing commissions were also party members. The composition of the new Supreme Soviet, and its newly-established parent body, the Congress of People's Deputies, is likely to be affected by the constitutional changes which are in the process of implementation at the time of writing. However, it is the party which will continue to provide political leadership and guidance in all state activities. The mandates of the standing commissions are very broad. Their role in the legislative process has been dealt with in the previous chapter. They may undertake any investigation within their subject mandate, including the examination of the operations of a public institution. They may travel in order to study a problem on the spot, seek the advice of experts, listen to the concerns of ordinary people, and make recommendations for the resolution of problems or the improvement of working efficiency. The activities of standing commissions of both chambers and of committees of the Supreme Soviet as a whole are co-ordinated by the Presidium.

The National People's Congress of China appoints a number of special committees, some permanent, some provisional. There are six permanent committees, specifically the Nationalities Committee, charged with the special responsibility of strengthening unity among different nationalities; the Law Committee; Financial and Economic Committee; Foreign Affairs Committee; Overseas Chinese Committee; and a committee with a very broad mandate covering education, science, culture and public health. Provisional committees are appointed to undertake inquiries into specific issues. These committees have multifarious responsibilities, including the examination of bills and other proposals emanating from the National People's Congress or its Standing Committee. The Law Committee has the special responsibility of examining all draft laws on a unified basis, relating them and their implications to the body of law as a whole. The special committees can also initiate their own draft laws and resolutions. Other functions include the examination of administrative regulations, decrees and directives and the consideration of responses given by organs of the state to inquiries directed to them by the National People's Congress, its Standing Committee and special committees. The Standing Committee appoints a Credentials Committee from among its own members, its function being to examine the credentials of the members of the National People's Congress and report on the validity of their election.

Recent developments in Bulgaria have strengthened the committee structure of the National Assembly, one innovation being the creation of a committee to deal with the rights of the citizen. It operates like a collective ombudsman, and while its status has yet to be finalised, it is likely that its functions will be widened. Citizens can make submissions orally or in writing to the committee which makes representations to the competent authority. The National Assembly can appoint as many committees as it likes. They oversee the operation of ministries and other government agencies, but recently their functions have been extended to enable them to deal with their subject mandates on a global basis. A Legislative Committee of 22 members is responsible for the drafting of bills. The other committees may also draft bills for submission to the Legislative Committee, which is obliged to consider any drafts referred to it. In 1986 the rules of the National Assembly were amended to empower committees to compel public organisations to apply recommendations issuing from the former.

Committees have a crucial role to play in most of the socialist countries, although it is difficult to assess the varying degrees of their importance within each system. Since the Parliaments of these countries meet in plenary session only for periods of short duration, it is a fair assumption that the major proportion of the ongoing work is carried out by committees in most cases. It is understood that most of the important work of Hungary's National Assembly is dealt with by its committees; and even in Romania, a country with a particularly rigid power structure, the functions and responsibilities of the committees of the Grand National Assembly have increased markedly in recent years.

The Importance of Parliamentary Committees

It is often said that the best way to shelve an embarrassing issue is to refer it to a committee. No doubt this is an expedient which has been employed on many occasions in many jurisdictions. It is also said that solutions arrived at by compromise are not always realistic solutions. If a committee were called upon to invent an animal, so say the cynics, it would probably have a camel's hump, an elephant's trunk, a giraffe's neck and a centipede's legs. These, of course, are one-sided assessments. It is true that a small committee is more likely to get things done than a large one. However, the effectiveness of any committee must be judged by the nature of its task and the way in which it fulfils its mandate. Parliamentary committees are essential to the success of any system of government. Within the infinite volume of committee records spread throughout the Parliaments of the world are to be found repositories of wisdom, scholarship, information and the fruits of wide-ranging study and research. Occasionally committees offer solutions to problems, sometimes they simply identify them, very frequently they make proposals or recommendations which may or may not prove effective. Sometimes their proposals are acted upon, sometimes they are rejected, at other times simply ignored. On occasion the influence of a committee's work emerges only with time. Some investigatory committees expose abuses. Committees also play their part in refining and improving legislation. It is not always possible to exclude partisanship from committee work, but it is frequently far more subdued, and co-operation and common purpose between political adversaries is by no means unusual when working together in a committee. The evidence indicates that the contribution of committees to the parliamentary process is positive and of incalculable value. Few Parliaments, even among the smallest, would be able to operate without them.

Notes

1 This committee consists of ten members of the House and ten of the Belgian members of the European Parliament.
2 Both the Senate and the Chamber of Deputies will, in exceptional circumstances, deal with a bill in committee of the whole House if it is necessary to expedite its passage.

7 Parliamentary Immunities

Parliamentary immunities are accorded to members of Parliament to provide them with the protection they need to enable them to fulfil their duties without fear of reprisals. Freedom of speech and voting is a fundamental right of all parliamentarians and is constitutionally or legally guaranteed in virtually all jurisdictions. As a general principle it can be stated that members of Parliament everywhere are immune from civil or criminal prosecution in respect of anything they say in the course of debate in the House or its committees. They are equally protected from molestation when pursuing their legitimate parliamentary activities, any violation of this right usually being punishable either by the courts or by Parliament itself. Threats, intimidation, harassment, bribery attempts and physical obstruction of a member attending to his or her parliamentary duties are examples of the kind of molestation from which members have the right to be protected. It is only realistic to add that in countries where the law permits of preventive detention without trial, the value of parliamentary immunity is likely to be questioned. The incarceration of political dissidents with no reason specified is not unknown in the world, and members of Parliament are sometimes among the victims.[1]

In the parliamentary vocabulary the words 'privilege' and 'immunity' are sometimes used synonymously. In some jurisdictions a clear distinction is made between the two terms. In Israel, for example, members enjoy certain rights under the law which are termed privileges, and certain exemptions from the ordinary law which are called immunities. In Egypt privileges are rights which are not related to public order, whereas immunities, which include freedom from arrest and criminal prosecution, are related to public order. In many countries, including Austria, Belgium, Finland, France, West Germany and the Netherlands, 'parliamentary privilege' would be considered an inappropriate expression, although the protection afforded to members in some jurisdictions is quite extensive.

'Parliamentary privilege' is a term which, for historic reasons, has a deep significance in the British Parliament and as a result has gained currency in most Commonwealth Parliaments. It has been recognised, however, that it is an expression which tends to be misleading. Privilege is not granted to parliamentarians in order to confer on them benefits which are not enjoyed by their fellow-citizens. It is given to them exclusively to enable them to perform their duties without let or hindrance and is therefore not privilege in a personal sense. A select committee of the British House of Commons, reporting in 1967, proposed that the term 'rights and immunities' should be substituted for 'parliamentary privilege' in order to eliminate the possibility of confusion in the public mind.

The history of parliamentary privilege in Great Britain is inextricably woven into the constitutional history of that country. It parallels the fierce and prolonged struggle waged by the Commons against the Crown to win the rights and freedoms which are enjoyed today. It is founded in the common law and the privilege of freedom of speech was confirmed by the Bill of Rights of 1689, a great constitutional milestone, which declared, *inter alia*, 'That the freedom of speech and debates or proceedings in Parliament ought not to be impeached or questioned in any court or place out of Parliament'. The privilege had, of course, been regularly claimed centuries before the enactment of the Bill of Rights. To this day, at the commencement of every Parliament, the Speaker, following his election, lays claim on behalf of the Commons at the bar of the House of Lords 'by humble petition to their ancient and undoubted rights and privileges', notable among which are freedom of speech and freedom from arrest. Most Commonwealth countries have been influenced by British practice and have made similar provision for parliamentary privilege in their constitutions and by statute. In these countries, and in certain others including Denmark, Ireland, Japan, Jordan and the Netherlands, members are immune from the laws of defamation for anything they may say in the parliamentary chamber or its committees, but not outside Parliament. In Italy legal proceedings may be taken against a member for words spoken outside Parliament provided the House concerned gives its authorisation, although it has usually been held that opinions expressed orally or in writing fall within the exercise of a member's parliamentary duties. However, a recent case has led to the argument that there is a conflict of powers between Parliament and the courts because the constitution did not exclude the jurisdiction of the courts. At the time of writing the matter awaits adjudication by the Constitutional Court. In Egypt, France and Israel the immunity extends to words spoken outside Parliament when related to the discharge of a member's parliamentary duties.

Under British practice, the privilege of freedom from arrest has never applied to arrest on criminal charges. In the days when imprisonment for debt was not uncommon, it was a privilege of some significance, but it has ceased to have much importance today. Most

Commonwealth countries follow British practice in according the privilege of freedom of arrest to parliamentarians in civil matters only, but in Malaysia, Mauritius and Zimbabwe, and also in the Netherlands, members are not immune from arrest in respect of any prosecution, civil or criminal. In some Parliaments, that of West Germany being an example, members are immune from arrest in both criminal and civil actions. In certain others they enjoy immunity in respect of criminal but not civil proceedings, this being the case in most Western European and socialist countries. In Finland, a limited immunity is available in criminal cases, and members are protected from arrest and prosecution provided they act according to justice and truth, a statutory provision which presumably only the courts could interpret. In Switzerland members enjoy relative immunity in respect of violations of the criminal law committed in the course of their parliamentary activities. No member may be prosecuted without the authorisation of both chambers. If a prosecution is authorised the chambers appoint a general prosecutor and the member is tried by the Federal Tribunal. The United States follows British practice in providing immunity from arrest in civil actions but not criminal cases. However, various judicial interpretations of the constitutional provision that 'for any Speech or Debate in either House, they (senators and congressmen) shall not be questioned in any other Place' have had the effect of quashing criminal proceedings in cases where a member is found to be 'acting in the sphere of legitimate legislative activity.'

In most countries where members are immune from arrest on criminal charges, an exception is made in cases of *flagrante delicto*. To effect an arrest within the precincts of Parliament itself usually requires the authority of the House or its presiding officer, an exception being the Netherlands where no such permission is required. Attempting to serve process on a member within the precincts of Parliament constitutes a violation of parliamentary immunity in most jurisdictions. In France the person of a member is protected beyond as well as within parliamentary precincts, although Parliament can waive this immunity. Even when Parliament is not sitting no member may be arrested or prosecuted for a criminal offence without the authorisation of the Bureau of the House of which he or she is a member, except in a case of *flagrante delicto*, if a prosecution had previously been initiated or a conviction already registered. In most countries where members are immune from criminal proceedings this immunity can be waived by the authority of Parliament. Members must expect to be held responsible for their actions like anybody else, and the concept of 'inviolability', in those countries where it exists, attaches to the office rather than the individual. In France it does not apply in civil cases or minor offences

119

such as traffic violations. Parliamentarians are usually exempted from jury service and from appearing in court as witnesses, although this latter immunity is frequently waived in the interests of justice. The principle underlying these immunities is that the parliamentary duties of members take priority over all else and they must be available to attend to them.

The constitutions of the socialist states guarantee similar immunities to their deputies as those to be found elsewhere, although the concept of parliamentary privilege as understood in Great Britain, the other Commonwealth countries and the United States is unknown. The constitution of the Soviet Union states that 'Deputies shall be ensured conditions for the unhampered and effective exercise of their rights and duties' and various legislative acts define their immunities. The consent of the Supreme Soviet is necessary before a member can be arrested, criminally prosecuted or subjected to measures of administrative punishment imposed by court orders.

Breaches of privilege or violations of parliamentary immunity are punishable offences in many countries. In some, such offences are left to the judgement of the courts. In others, Parliament itself claims the right to judge and to punish. The penal jurisdiction of both Houses of the British Parliament is an inherent power which has been inherited by most of the Parliaments of the Commonwealth. Parliamentary privilege has never been precisely defined in Commonwealth countries as their Parliaments have always jealously guarded the right to determine whether or not their privileges have been breached. Allied to parliamentary privilege is the offence of contempt, which covers a variety of acts which might tend to bring Parliament and its members into disrepute, diminish their authority or obstruct or impede them in any way in the performance of their functions. The limits of what constitutes a contempt are very vague.[2] It has not been unusual, for example, to raise as matters of privilege articles written by journalists or other publications which are alleged to defame Parliament. However, the boundary between fair comment and excessively strong criticism which might technically constitute a contempt is very thin as most Commonwealth Parliaments recognise. For many years the British Parliament has been extremely hesitant to invoke its penal powers, and the Canadian Parliament almost never proceeds against journalists, whatever they may write, in the interests of safeguarding the freedom of the press. There have been some cases in recent years, notably in Malta and Zambia, indicating that some Parliaments are more sensitive to derogatory criticism than others. One offence of which the British Parliament takes a particularly serious view is the unauthorised leaking of confidential committee proceedings.

In Australia the Parliamentary Privileges Act of 1987 abolished the power of both Houses of Parliament to punish people for defamation of parliamentarians and removed their power to expel their own members. Resolutions subsequently adopted in 1988 were aimed at protecting private citizens from unfair attacks made upon them by parliamentarians under cover of parliamentary privilege and protecting witnesses giving evidence before parliamentary committees.

When Parliament does impose a punishment, it normally takes the form of a reprimand administered by the presiding officer. If the offender is a member, it is received by the member standing in his or her place. If a non-member, the offender is required to appear at the bar of the House. The right to punish also includes the power to commit to prison for limited periods. Although it is very rarely invoked these days, it cannot be described as obsolete. As recently as 1955 the Australian House of Representatives sentenced two journalists to three months imprisonment for publishing scurrilous allegations against certain members of Parliament, although in the light of the recent legislation such a case could not arise again. Some Parliaments have the power to impose fines, although not, it would seem, the British House of Commons. Parliaments can in many cases expel their own members, and such action is usually taken if a member is convicted and sentenced to prison for a serious criminal offence. In 1947 the British House of Commons expelled one of its members after finding him guilty of a gross breach of privilege. When a serious case of privilege arises, it is usually referred to the appropriate committee and the House takes no action until the committee has reported.

In the United States the power of Congress to punish is more limited than it is in Great Britain and certain other Commonwealth countries. The constitution empowers the Congress to proceed against persons who offend against the clearly stated privileges of both Houses, as, for example, in the case of a person who deliberately attempts to obstruct a member in the fulfilment of his or her legislative duties. Congressional committees, all of which now have the power of subpoena, can also proceed against witnesses who refuse to co-operate, with the proviso that they cannot be forced to incriminate themselves. Congress does not, however, have a general power to punish for contempt and to determine for itself whether a particular act constitutes a contempt or not. The courts have a more direct involvement in the determination of such matters than would be the case in the British or other comparable Parliaments. In Great Britain, and most other Commonwealth countries, the courts recognise the exclusive jurisdiction of Parliament in matters of privilege, but conflicts have arisen between Parliament and the courts in cases where the limits of privilege have to be determined. If, for example, parliamentary privilege is invoked as a defence in a case before the courts, it is the court which decides whether the argument is acceptable or not.

In a number of other countries the power to punish violations of a member's parliamentary immunity is vested in the courts. This is the case in Austria, Belgium, Denmark, France, West Germany, Iceland, Israel, Japan, Monaco, the Netherlands and Sweden. In Italy the courts may adjudicate if so authorised by Parliament. In Israel the laying of a charge requires the permission of the *Knesset*. In Japan the process of indictment takes place in Parliament, the courts being left to judge the case. In West Germany Parliament can initiate proceedings and authorise prosecutions. In France and Belgium an offence against Parliament is dealt with in the same way as an offence against any other public authority. French legislation relating to Parliament does not incorporate the notion of an offence against Parliament as such. However, as in many other assemblies, a deputy may be temporarily excluded from the National Assembly by resolution of the House if guilty of a gross breach of order. In Finland, it would seem that violations of parliamentary immunity are not treated as offences so that the question of judging them does not arise. In the Soviet Union and other socialist countries, the concept of an offence against Parliament as such is unknown. The Soviet penal code makes no provision for punishing a violation of parliamentary immunity.

Parliamentary immunity is an exemption from the application of the law in circumstances where it is warranted by the need to protect parliamentarians in the fulfilment of their duties. Its extent varies from country to country, so that it is easier to generalise as to its purpose than as to how the need is viewed in different jurisdictions.

Notes

1 Many countries hold political prisoners and it is not the intention to single out any for special reproach. It must be remembered also that the power of preventive detention often existed in colonial territories long before the same colonies became independent nations.
2 Although the Australian Parliamentary Privileges Act of 1987 went some way towards defining what constitutes a contempt of Parliament.

8 Staff and Services

No consideration of the activities of Parliaments should fail to take into account the working conditions of members. To operate effectively, they need the support of staff, services, facilities and sources of information, and there is a wide disparity among Parliaments regarding the extent to which these are available. The salaries and emoluments of parliamentarians also vary widely, not surprisingly since economic conditions and standards of living vary from country to country. Furthermore, membership of Parliament is a full-time job in some countries but not in others. Some members in some Parliaments depend on their parliamentary incomes, in which case they need to be sufficient to provide a reasonable livelihood, but not such as to attract parliamentary candidates for the money alone. In some countries, such as the United States, legislators are generously remunerated. In others, such as the Soviet Union, membership of Parliament is not regarded as a profession in its own right and members continue to draw the salaries or wages attaching to their normal occupations.

It is impossible to generalise about the staffing of a Parliament. Some Parliaments employ large full-time staffs, and further staff may be available at other levels. In the United States Congress, for example, every senator and congressman has a personal staff; every committee hires its own independent staff, some being appointed by the majority and some by the minority; the Congressional Research Service, which is a division of the Library of Congress serving Congress directly, employs a large professional and support staff quite distinct from the separate establishments of the Senate and the House of Representatives. At the other end of the scale are many very small Parliaments with few if any full-time staff and very little in the way of other facilities.

Most Parliaments are likely to have a chief executive officer variously styled the Clerk of the House (the designation common to many Commonwealth Parliaments), Secretary-General or Director-General. The National Assembly of Bulgaria is one which does not have a Secretary-General. The Council of State has overall administrative responsibility for the Assembly, but the future of the

Council of State is currently under study and changes may result from the reforms which are under consideration at the time of writing. In bicameral Parliaments each House is likely to have its own chief executive, although in some this officer has joint authority over the staff of both, as in Austria, Jordan, Switzerland,[1] Thailand and Zimbabwe. Usually the parliamentary staff are independent of the public service, although in some Parliaments, notably the smaller ones, they are drawn from the public service. Interchangeability with the public service is important in countries where the parliamentary service offers only limited career prospects. The personnel of the secretariat of Thailand's bicameral National Assembly were civil servants until 1975, when their status was changed by law.

The chief executive officer is likely to have both administrative and procedural responsibilities. The duties of the position usually include the custody of the records of the House, financial administration, control of personnel (recruitment, promotion, discipline, assignment of duties, etc.), and advising the presiding officer and members generally on matters of parliamentary procedure, a field in which the incumbent is likely to be an expert.[2] In New Zealand the functions of the Clerk are defined in the Clerk of the House of Representatives Act, 1988, and are confined to the management of the Clerk's own establishment and the provision of professional services to the House and its committees, and to members engaged in inter-parliamentary activities. The Parliamentary Service, under the direction of a General Manager, is responsible for the provision of other services and facilities to members, together with administrative and support services to the Office of the Clerk. In Thailand the Secretary-General controls a staff of some 500 people, distributed among a wide range of divisions and sections in the administrative, procedural and technical fields. In Austria the Director of Parliament heads an office which employs about 240 people within five departments or *dienste*. These are the *Nationalratsdienst* which provides organisational and pro-cedural services to the lower House; the *Bundesratsdienst* which provides similar services to the upper House as well as joint services to both Houses; the Legal and Administrative Service; the Parliamen-tary Record Department and Press Release Service; and the Parlia-mentary Research Service which includes the Parliamentary Library and a wide range of documentation services.

In most Parliaments the status of the position equates to that of a permanent head of a government department. In some it is lower down the scale, in others even higher. In Zambia, for example, the Clerk of the National Assembly has the status of a supreme court judge. In some countries this officer is elected by the Parliament, this being the case in the Swedish *Riksdag* and in the respective Houses of the Japanese Diet and the US Congress. In a number of countries the presiding officer or bureau is empowered to make the appointment. In Great Britain and certain Commonwealth countries, it is made under the authority of the head of state following consultation. Tenure of the office is usually permanent, although the incumbent is removable for cause, but in the US Congress the Secretary of the Senate and the Clerk of the House of Representatives are liable to be replaced should the majority change in the House concerned. In Malawi and other countries where the parliamentary staff are integrated with the public service, they are all, including the chief officer, liable to transfer to government departments.

In small Parliaments the chief officer is likely to carry much of the work-load personally. In large Parliaments he or she will probably control a considerable staff, including a substantial complement of professional officers, grouped into departments each with its own director. Committees must be serviced, records must be maintained, essential information, advice and assistance must always be available to parliamentarians in every area of parliamentary activity. Administrative services are required to provide and monitor the facilities needed by members, which are likely to include office accommodation and equipment, transport, telephone and mailing privileges, catering services, secretarial and messenger services, and the provision of parliamentary publications. Not all parliamentarians, even in larger Parliaments, have their own private offices and personal staffs. Canadian parliamentarians are among those who enjoy these amenities, and their emoluments include a tax-free expense allowance.

Parliamentarians in small Parliaments are often called upon to do their job with limited assistance and very few facilities. The Leader of the Opposition in a small Commonwealth Parliament recently confided to the author that Parliament provided him with no office accommodation or secretarial assistance and that he was obliged to use his own private office and secretary to do his parliamentary work. He also complained that he could seldom obtain information from government departments because public servants were apprehensive of the reaction of ministers if they were seen to be helping the opposition.

In no area is the gulf between rich and poor Parliaments more evident than in the facilities available for providing information and research services to parliamentarians. Some Parliaments are richly endowed with such services, the US Congress and the Japanese Diet probably leading the field, and Australia, Brazil, Great Britain, Canada, France, West Germany, India, Italy, South Korea and Sweden, being among the countries where extensive and sophisticated services are available. Almost every Parliament has a parliamentary library, varying in size and quality. Bicameral Parliaments often have one library providing joint services, although in Great Britain, France, West Germany and Italy each House of Parliament has its own separate library. In some Parliaments the library and the research and documentation services are separately administered, but in most jurisdictions they are integrated. Even the smallest Parliaments usually have a library of sorts, amounting sometimes only to a small collection of books. Some of them may even appoint a librarian, but such an appointment is often a luxury. The richer parliamentary libraries, by contrast, are normally well staffed, not only by librarians but also by other professionals in a wide range of disciplines who provide research and expert advice to their parliamentary clients. Most major parliamentary libraries have computerised services and access to data banks. In these Parliaments, the chief librarian is almost certain to be a very senior officer. In the United States the Congressional Research Service, although a department of the Library of Congress which is the national library, is separately administered under its own director. It has its own library and a range of subject divisions, its staff includes specialists of international repute, and it offers an impressive range of services to both Houses of Congress, their members and committees.

Apart from the National People's Congress of China and the Great People's *Khural* of Mongolia, which do not have libraries of their own,[3] the assemblies of the socialist states have parliamentary libraries providing various services and staffed by librarians and others. In the Soviet Union the parliamentary library forms part of the Presidium secretariat, and although its holdings are not as large as those of some of the parliamentary libraries elsewhere, a very large staff is employed in the provision of documentation, research and reference services. The most important sources of information for deputies in the socialist states are government departments and agencies, and other state-supported organisations, all of which have a legal obligation to respond to requests from parliamentary commissions and individual deputies.

In 1973 a symposium was organised in Geneva by the Inter-Parliamentary Union on the theme: 'The Member of Parliament: His Requirements for Information in the Modern World'. Although the delegates represented countries from all regions of the world and many different political systems, they discovered a great deal of common ground through their shared experiences. There was general agreement that parliamentarians did not suffer from a shortage of information but rather too much of it. The problem lay in making effective use of the information available through judicious selection, analysis and interpretation. The role of experts and other services designed to assist members was considered in depth, and there was general agreement that too heavy a reliance on experts could lead to serious risks, not the least of which was the risk of the expert becoming the directing force behind the member. As one delegate pointed out, experts at one time or another had predicted that the *Titanic* could not sink, that Picasso could not paint and that gold would never rise above 40 dollars an ounce and they therefore could not be considered infallible. It was for the elected member to listen to the views of experts, which were often conflicting, and to bring his or her own independent judgement to bear on the issue.

At this symposium the delegates from the socialist countries placed great stress on the extensive services available to deputies through government sources. Delegates from some of the other countries took the view that in order to be well-informed a member needed many different sources of information, including those independent of government control. Delegates from some third world countries, while lamenting the fact that lack of financial resources prevented them from establishing the services available in wealthier nations, emphasised the importance of the oral tradition of communicating information. There was general agreement that direct contact between the member and the electors was indispensable to the learning process, and oral communication was particularly essential in countries where there was widespread illiteracy.

Parliamentary staff as well as parliamentarians derive great benefits from conferences, seminars and symposia of the kind described above. Parliamentary associations such as the Inter-Parliamentary Union, the Commonwealth Parliamentary Association and the International Association of French-speaking Parliamentarians, provide regular opportunities for such meetings, both internationally and regionally. Among other institutions serving as forums for international consultation and discussion among parliamentarians are the Council of Europe, the Western European Union, the African Union of Parliaments, the Arab Inter-Parliamentary Union, the Latin American Parliament, the Andean Parliament and the North Atlantic Assembly, bodies sharing regional, linguistic or ethnic interests. The only example so far of a supra-national Parliament, directly elected by the people and participating in the decision-making process, is the European Parliament which serves the interests of the European Economic Community.

Allied to the three associations first mentioned are the Association of Secretaries-General of Parliaments, the Society of Clerks-at-the-Table in Commonwealth Parliaments and the Association of Secretaries-General of French-speaking Parliaments which are professional associations of parliamentary officers. The matters discussed at their meetings relate to parliamentary practice and administration, and problems and issues of common concern to those who serve

Parliaments. For some years a Parliamentary Libraries Section has operated within the Division of General Research Libraries of the International Federation of Library Associations. Its aims are to improve parliamentary library services throughout the world and promote communication and co-operation among parliamentary libraries and between parliamentary libraries and other organisations. In August 1987 the first meeting of Commonwealth Parliamentary Librarians was held in London to discuss methods of improving information and research services to parliamentarians. These meetings of professional practitioners have led to a sense of fraternity amongst them, transcending differing political ideologies and conflicts between nations. Their value could hardly be exaggerated.

Notes

1　It is interesting to note that in Switzerland each parliamentary party has its own secretariat financed from public funds and these services fall under the jurisdiction of the Secretary-General of the Federal Assembly.
2　In both Houses of the U.S. Congress the procedural expert is an officer styled the Parliamentarian. The Secretary of the Senate and the Clerk of the House of Representatives are the chief officers with administrative and a wide range of other duties.
3　Deputies of the Great People's *Khural* have access to a government library located in the same building.

9   Parliament and its Public Relations

Parliament and the Media

In the British House of Commons daily prayers are said at the commencement of each sitting by the Speaker's Chaplain, and there is an old parliamentary joke to the effect that he looks at the assembled members and prays for the country. The Yugoslavs have a joke of their own. Their parliamentary building is surmounted by a dome, and when visitors ask why there is a dome, they reply: 'Have you ever seen a circus without a dome?' Parliaments are ready-made targets for criticism and their image is probably something less than ideal in most countries. Their activities are followed more closely than ever before by the public and the media. Being human institutions they are not always seen at their best. When they rise to great occasions and debate is statesmanlike, they can justly claim to function as the grand forum of the nation. When tempers fray and the proceedings degenerate into rowdiness and name-calling their human weaknesses are revealed. The media are ever present to report what they believe is worth reporting, and through the most powerful of all the media, television, the moods of Parliament and the behaviour of its members can be relentlessly exposed. Much of the proceedings of Parliament may seem dull from the point of view of the public, and the media, for obvious reasons, seek headlines and highlights. This is not to say that media coverage of Parliament is never objective, but a member who says or does something outrageous is more assured of a headline than one who makes a constructive speech. It is thus the great occasions on the one hand and the petty confrontations on the other which tend to capture the attention of the media and the public. Debates on the more significant measures and issues are likely to be summarised in the so-called 'serious' newspapers, the entire proceedings being recorded only in Parliament's own official publications.

The relationship between Parliament and the media is often an adversarial one. This can be so even in a one-party state where the media are government-controlled. In Zambia, for example, the press regularly comes into conflict with the National Assembly over what is seen by the latter as unwarranted criticism. It could be that this parliamentary sensitivity reflects the assertion by the National Assembly of its independence in the face of possible encroachment by the executive and party authorities. But regardless of such conflicts, and Zambia is far from being the only country where they occur, Parliament and the media are inseparable bedfellows. Cooperation between them is indispensable in order to protect the public's right to know and provide parliamentarians with the publicity on which they depend, even though some of it is adverse. For this reason Parliaments invariably provide the media with the facilities they need.

All Parliaments reserve gallery space for journalists where they are allowed to take notes. In many Parliaments special rooms are provided for the use of the media, and interviewing and broadcasting facilities are also sometimes made available. In Israel the *Knesset* provides foreign reporters with equipment for direct transmission to their own countries. In some Parliaments general access to the facilities of the building is almost unrestricted. In Australia and Canada, for example, accredited members of the press gallery have the use of the parliamentary library and the members' restaurant. In the British Parliament parliamentary correspondents do not have unrestricted access to the library and other facilities of the building, but they have their own press gallery accommodation and services. Special privileges are accorded to a select group of senior journalists known as lobby correspondents. They are the only media representatives allowed the right of entry to the Members' Lobby in the House of Commons and the Peers' Lobby in the House of Lords. Similarly in India, selected media representatives have access to the central lobby of the parliamentary building. In the United States the Speaker of the House of Representatives holds a daily press conference. Senators and congressmen make statements and furnish documents to the press as they see fit, and congressional staff are assigned to the press galleries. In Yugoslavia arrangements are made for daily contacts between deputies and accredited journalists. Facilities for holding press conferences and the issuance of regular press releases are services provided by numerous Parliaments.

It is within the authority of any parliamentary chamber to withdraw press privileges in cases of impropriety. However, most Parliaments, in view of the importance they attach to their public relations, would be reluctant to take such action. It is noteworthy that in 1975 the British House of Commons declined to impose this sanction in the case of a weekly newspaper which had prematurely leaked the contents of a select committee report, believing that the public would suffer more than the newspaper if the latter were deprived of its means of reporting on parliamentary affairs.

Parliamentary Information Services

Parliaments throughout the world are more conscious than ever before of their duty to keep the public informed. Walter Bagehot, writing as long ago as 1867, laid stress on the 'teaching' function of the British House of Commons, and the responsibility it has 'to express the mind of the English people on all matters which come before it.'[1] Many more matters come before Parliaments today than when Bagehot wrote those words, and far more attention is paid to the public's right to know. Records have been kept by Parliaments for many years, in some cases for centuries. Verbatim reports of debates, evidence given before committees, and a host of reports and other documents are published and made available to the public in the great majority of Parliaments. The fact remains that these official publications have only a limited readership, and in many jurisdictions they are no longer regarded as sufficient to keep the public properly informed. The ever-widening range of government responsibilities ensures that there are few areas of public activity which do not claim the attention of Parliaments. The technological age and the resulting information explosion, if one may be pardoned for using these clichés, have transformed parliamentary life. One result has been the establishment of public information services in a number of Parliaments.

The Belgian House of Representatives has an office which translates into English as the Division of Protocol and Public Relations. The Indian House of the People has a Press and Public Relations section, and similar offices are to be found in the West German *Bundestag* and the Second Chamber of the Netherlands Parliament. One of the divisions of the Secretariat of Thailand's bicameral National Assembly is responsible for public relations and it includes a Mass Media Relations Section. A Public Information Office was created in the library of the British House of Commons in 1978 and shortly afterwards an Education Officer was appointed to the library staff to provide a parliamentary educational service for schools. In the House of Lords the provision of information to the public is the responsibility of the Journal and Information Office which also compiles the journals recording the proceedings of the House. The Australian Parliament recently established a Parliamentary Education Office under the joint direction of both Houses. Its efforts are aimed principally at schools and students and it works in co-operation with teachers and curriculum consultants, a project officer with this professional background having been appointed in 1985. The office produces information kits and other materials and arranges group visits to the Parliament itself. The Joint House Department also provides a range of services and publications to the visiting public at large. The Canadian House of Commons estab-lished a Public Information Office in 1988. Both the Australian and Canadian Parliaments hire parliamentary guides who are trained to take visitors on conducted tours through the buildings. Public relations initiatives have also been taken in some of the younger Parliaments. Shortly after Zimbabwe became independent in 1980, it was decided that if Parliament was to be meaningful to the people, a public information service was required and an Information Office was established. In countries which have emerged from colonialism, Parliaments can easily be seen as alien institutions. Adaptations are necessary to meet the needs of the societies which they serve, societies which in pre-colonial days frequently had their own representative systems. An effective parliamentary information service provides a valuable bridge between the people and their representative institutions.

Some Parliaments publish bulletins designed for a popular reader-ship, such as the Weekly Information Bulletin of the Public Informa-tion Office of the British House of Commons. In Mongolia the Presidium of the Great People's *Khural* publishes a magazine entitled 'People's State' which provides information on that assembly's activities. The Congressional Research Service in Washington issues a number of publications which are available to the public. It also responds directly to inquiries from the public by sending out background papers and other readily available material on a wide range of subjects. The Supreme Soviet of the USSR provides an information service which publishes a Gazette and issues press releases and communiqués on its various activities. The library of the General Assembly of New Zealand serves government departments and the general public as well as parliamentarians. It also has a specific obligation to make available any materials collected under international exchange agreements and deposit arrangements to anybody who needs them. In some countries the public's right to know has been recognised by the adoption of legislation guarantee-ing freedom of information. Australia, Canada, Sweden and the United States have been very progressive in this field, and in Sweden the law even requires the public release of research papers prepared for parliamentarians, should they be demanded. In most Parliaments where research services are provided for members, this requirement would be seen as a severe limitation of their value, the element of confidentiality being an important aspect of such services in most cases.

Broadcasting of Parliamentary Proceedings

Of the many technological developments which have transformed modern living, none has had a greater impact on the conduct of public affairs than broadcasting, and in particular television broadcasting. Parliaments throughout the world have wrestled with the question of whether or not to allow the television cameras into the chamber. Many have done so, but many more continue to hesitate or may not even have considered it. Radio broadcasting of parliamentary proceedings has proved less controversial, and the New Zealand Parliament was a pioneer in this field, having introduced it in the House of Representatives as long ago as 1936. In the following year continuous broadcasting of the proceedings was instituted, and New Zealand became the first country in the Commonwealth, if not in the world, to take this step. In 1946 Australia introduced sound broadcasting of the debates in both Houses of Parliament, the broadcasts being governed by statute and controlled by a joint committee of both Houses. Regular sound broadcasting of the proceedings of both Houses of the British Parliament was introduced in 1978. The Parliament of the Solomon Islands is one of the smaller Parliaments whose proceedings are broadcast live by radio.

Television, being a visual medium, reveals a great deal more than sound alone. The arguments for and against televising Parliament have been exhausted both in parliamentary debate, in committee studies and in published articles. They need not concern us here, except that one point needs to be emphasised. If Parliament does not allow the cameras into the debating chamber, the reporting of its proceedings on television is left entirely in the hands of journalists, commentators, interviewers and experts, none of whom are answerable to an electorate. Television undoubtedly exposes the warts on the face of Parliament, but at least it is seen by the viewer as it really is and not simply as it is represented by others. The television camera in the chamber is an extension of the public gallery, bringing Parliament into the homes of all who care to tune in. It is always likely to transform parliamentary behaviour, whether for better or worse being in the hands of parliamentarians themselves. Television is a factor to be reckoned with in Parliament's public relations. Whatever Parliaments do, it is here to stay and cannot be ignored.

Of those Parliaments which have admitted the television cameras, only a few provide continuous live coverage of all the proceedings. Since 1977 the entire proceedings of the Canadian House of Commons have been broadcast by television and radio through a system owned and controlled by the House itself and operated by its own staff. The cameras must focus on the member who has the floor and are not allowed to pan. A complete electronic record of the debates is maintained and the media are free to select the material they wish to use. In the US Congress the entire proceedings of both Houses are telecast, the broadcasts being under the supervision of each House independently. Among the socialist countries, the proceedings of the National Assembly of Hungary are carried live and unabridged by radio and television, the operation being directed by the Government Information Office, which also supervises the selection of material by the media. In Bulgaria the National Assembly itself supervises the operation, and determines whether the entire proceedings or only a selection shall be broadcast. In China, Cuba, Mongolia and Poland, the media select the material to be used. In the Soviet Union the meetings of the newly elected Congress of People's Deputies were televised daily from their inception.

Some Parliaments leave the coverage of their proceedings entirely in the hands of the media, while others reserve their authority to grant permission. In Denmark, West Germany, Luxembourg and Sweden the media determine what shall be broadcast and there is no parliamentary involvement. In Norway no permission is required for radio broadcasts, but television broadcasts require the permission of the Secretary-General, which is readily granted. In Italy parliamentary broadcasts by the state broadcasting service require the permission of the presiding officer of the chamber concerned, but private radio broadcasts of full debates require no permission. In France authorisation is given by the Bureau of the House concerned, which must also be satisfied that the coverage provided is equitable. In Thailand the President of the House of Representatives is authorised to arrange for sound and television broadcasts of the proceedings. The President of the Senate may authorise sound broadcasts if he deems it expedient. Belgium, Egypt, Greece, Israel, Japan, South Korea, the Netherlands, Portugal and Switzerland are among other countries where the media carry out the operation and select the material to be used with the prior permission of the assembly or its presiding officer. In Costa Rica a major broadcasting company is contracted to broadcast parliamentary proceedings by radio in their entirety, partial coverage being provided by television.

In Malta the Speaker has the responsibility of deciding whether the proceedings should be televised or not, and is sometimes faced with conflicting opinions. On a recent occasion, government and opposition were unable to agree, one wanting full coverage and the other no coverage at all. The Speaker compromised by authorising partial coverage, transmissions taking place between 4.00 p.m. and 7.00 p.m. but not in prime time. The proceedings of Singapore's Parliament have been televised since 1985 and the cameras are allowed to pan. At the end of the day an edited version is broadcast and entitled 'Today in Parliament'.

In Great Britain television broadcasting was introduced experimentally in the House of Lords in 1985, and in 1988 it was agreed to by the House of Commons on an experimental basis. The issue had been debated over a long period, and on several previous occasions the House of Commons had turned down the proposal. It was decided, following investigation by a select committee, to commence television broadcasting in November 1989 under strictly controlled conditions.

Continuous live television coverage of a Parliament's proceedings will not of itself guarantee that the public will have a balanced view of Parliament. Since its advent in the Canadian House of Commons, for example, public attention has largely focused on the daily question period, a period of confrontation between the government and the opposition parties when parliamentary behaviour is seldom seen at its best. The House must therefore expect to be judged to a great extent by what goes on during this part of the parliamentary day.

Members and their Constituents

A well-informed electorate is just as important an element of good government as well-informed members of Parliament. The media certainly provide information, but they tend to inform selectively. In the overall context of Parliament and its public relations, there is no substitute for regular direct contact and communication between members of Parliament and those they represent. By this means the member can not only inform, but become informed. In the Soviet Union continual exchanges of views between the people and their representatives are regarded as the most valuable factors in organising a deputy's information needs. The revised constitution requires deputies to report on their work and on that of the Congress of People's Deputies, the Supreme Soviet or a local Soviet to their constituents, work collectives and social organisations. Provision is made for the recall of deputies who have not justified the confidence of their constituents. In some third world countries, where many people are poor and illiterate, and access to television sets is limited, the oral tradition of communication may well provide the only means whereby parliamentarians and the people can exchange information. In countries with greater advantages, the channels of communication are many, but it can be stated as a universal principle that no member of Parliament can afford to neglect his or her constituency. A basic premise offered in the first chapter of this study is that one function common to all Parliaments is that of representation. Of the many duties of a parliamentarian, none is more important. There are some countries in which the media are always ready to comment when debates take place in a chamber with few members present. These observations usually overlook the fact that chamber duties are not the sum total of a member's responsibilities, and that a member's absence from the chamber does not mean that his or her parliamentary duties are being neglected. Members serve on committees and have public engagements to attend; they have correspondence to deal with; they must prepare for debates in which they intend to participate; and, of course, much of their work demands their physical presence in their electoral districts. Parliament belongs to the people and its evolution depends on its keeping in touch with the people. As an institution it has shown itself to be infinitely adaptable, and adapt it must if it is to remain effective. Perhaps, as was suggested by Mr. André Chandernagor of France when presiding over the Inter-Parliamentary Union symposium of 1973, referred to in the previous chapter, the only true parliamentary tradition is that of adaptation.

Notes

1   Walter Bagehot, *The English Constitution*, Fontana/Collins, 1963, p.152.

10   Conclusion

Political philosophy is an ancient study, its extant writings taking us back to Plato and Aristotle, and many theories of government have been propounded throughout the ages. While the principle of universal suffrage is a modern concept, progressive thinkers have always underlined the importance of representative government and individual freedom in the context of their theories. Locke and Rousseau both saw government as a social contract in which all participated and accepted the will of the majority as the general will. The people, they argued, were free under the law when they themselves were the law-makers. De Tocqueville and John Stuart Mill, while recognising majority rule as the inescapable consequence of democratic government, had reservations about the possible tyranny of the majority, and were advocates of checks and balances. De Tocqueville greatly admired the principle of the separation of powers enshrined in the American constitution. Montesquieu, whose death pre-dated de Tocqueville's by a century, was also a believer in the separation of powers, but being mainly interested in liberty, had an inbred distrust of any form of organised government. Bentham took the view that any law was by definition an encroachment on personal liberty and was acceptable only when it clearly contributed to the general welfare. He believed that the legislative activities of Parliaments should be minimal and restricted to what was clearly necessary to the interests of society as a whole. Karl Marx advanced a totally different theory of government through his view of the contest for political power as a class struggle between the oppressors and the oppressed. At the time he wrote he believed that society had crystallised into two great hostile sections, the *bourgeoisie* and the proletariat. His road to democracy lay through revolution which would destroy capitalism and place the means of production in the hands of the people to be used for the common benefit.

Whether or not they be revolutionary in nature, modern theories of government invariably rest on the basic principles of the sovereignty of the people and the consent of the governed. In any system with a claim to legitimacy as 'government of the people, by the people, for the people', to borrow Lincoln's famous phrase, the representative assembly has a central role to play. Parliaments are the voice of the people in an increasingly complex world. Its complexity is reflected in the distribution of powers both within and among nations, a factor which constantly threatens to erode the powers of representative institutions. Significant powers touching the lives of ordinary people reside not only in bureaucratic institutions but also in bodies beyond the direct control of the normal electoral and legislative processes, such as multi-national corporations and supranational institutions created by power blocs and international alliances.

Fortunately there are signs throughout the world that both governments and the governed are acutely aware of the dangers inherent in the global pattern of power distribution. Small though the world may be in terms of its closely-knit relationships, there has been no lessening of national consciousness among nations. While recognising the practical advantages of economic or military inter-dependence, there are few countries which do not prize their political independence, and few peoples who would wish to see their national identity submerged. A country's national consciousness is reflected in its representative assembly, and the assertion of national identity frequently surfaces in the course of parliamentary debate. Parliament should embody the character of a nation. The right of the people to be consulted and to participate in the making of decisions which will affect them is becoming increasingly recognised. Parliaments, and governments too, are listening to the people, not only those who are experts in their particular fields, but the ordinary man and woman in the street as well. The use of parliamentary committees to take evidence from members of the public is a common practice in many countries. The referendum is another method of consulting public opinion and in Australia and Switzerland it is an essential feature in the process of constitutional amendment. Even in Great Britain, where the referendum had long been alien to that country's political traditions, referenda have been held on entry into the European Economic Community and the devolution of powers to Scotland and Wales. Of particular significance was the referendum held in Poland in 1987 on proposals for economic and political reform, which resulted in a defeat for the government. A plebiscite held in Chile in 1988 resulted in a vote of 54% to 43% against the continued dictatorship of General Pinochet, and although it did not bring an immediate end to his rule, the fact that it was held at all was an event in itself. In February 1989 a referendum was held in Algeria at which a new constitution was approved. Previously a one-party socialist state, Algeria seems likely to undergo a transformation of its political system. The new constitution will be far-reaching in its effects, and will allow the development of a multi-party system.

Participatory democracy can take various forms. Bodies such as Canada's Public Policy Forum provide a bridge between business and industry on the one hand and Parliament and the executive on the other. The conferences, seminars and projects organised by such groups promote consultation and co-operation between the public and private sectors and have an influence on the framing of public policy. Such contacts enable legislators and bureaucrats to appreciate the preoccupations of the private sector and the latter to understand better the processes involved in parliamentary government. At the academic level, associations such as Britain's Study of Parliament Group, which has inspired the creation of similar groups in other countries, pursue their aims by bringing the students of Parliament into contact with the practitioners, the parliamentary staff as well as the parliamentarians themselves. Academics well-versed in the theory of parliamentary government are given greater exposure to the way it works in practice. Parliamentarians for their part pay serious attention to the views of well-informed observers of the parliamentary scene.

To reap the full benefits of public consultation Parliament must play a crucial role in the decision-making process. Though some political scientists believe that Parliament is in decline, and select their evidence in order to demonstrate their thesis, global trends would seem to offer hope that this is not necessarily true. *Perestroika* in the Soviet Union is leading to a more representative electoral system and the greater effectiveness of Soviets at all levels in direct decision-making and the control of the bureaucracy. Significant reforms are taking place in Poland and Hungary paving the way for the formation of new parties and the free expression of dissent. Bulgaria, at the time of writing, is also embarking on a programme of reform which will include a new electoral law and the strengthening of the role of the National Assembly. A new standing committee of the Assembly dealing with the rights of the citizen has recently been set up, and consideration will be given to the establishment of a Constitutional Council to determine the constitutionality of laws. In those Western countries where party discipline is an important element in the operation of the parliamentary system, there is a consciousness of the need to introduce more flexibility into the system. In Canada, for example, recent procedural reforms have stressed the need to allow more independence to backbenchers, and strengthened the independence of committees by allowing them to initiate their own inquiries. Procedures described in previous chapters for calling the executive to account, and the public exposure of these proceedings through the broadcast media, can reinforce the influence of legislative bodies. Those who serve parliamentary institutions and are able to observe their operation at close quarters tend to be less impressed by the theory that Parliament is in decline.[1] Parliaments are human institutions and therefore not infallible. They should not be written off simply because they do not attain the utopian ideals which some theorists set for them. Some commentators have even been known to lament the loss of powers which Parliaments never had in the first place. Perhaps the process of strengthening Parliament has not gone far enough, but the importance of an effective Parliament in a truly representative system of government is widely recognised.

Victor Hugo defined *'le parlementarisme'* in a flourish of words which may be freely paraphrased as the citizens' guarantee of freedom of speech, freedom of the press, individual freedom, freedom of conscience, freedom of religion, control of public finance, personal security, protection against arbitrary government and the dignity of the nation. At the time he wrote he maintained that it had ceased to exist in France, the legislative body having become impotent. Were he alive today he might be agreeably surprised at the extent of the revival of *'le parlementarisme'* not only in his own country but throughout the world. Many Parliaments come together under the umbrella of the Inter-Parliamentary Union and there are many differences between them. Not all the systems of government in which they operate embody the totality of Hugo's definition. But in judging an institution, as in judging a nation or an individual, we should perhaps judge it not only by its actual achievements, its successes and failures, but also by the ideals to which it aspires.

Parliaments throughout the world have undergone radical changes since the Inter-Parliamentary Union was founded in 1889. In the course of the century many new ones have been created, while others have ceased to exist. Many national boundaries have been redrawn, systems of government have changed in many countries, and it is a virtual certainty that in no country in the world have the institutions of government remained unchanged by the events of the past 100 years. What the next 100 years will bring is anybody's guess. But whether they be years of upheaval or years of tranquillity, parliamentary institutions will continue to evolve and adapt to changing circumstances. This, as Mr. Chandernagor reminded us, is the ongoing tradition of Parliament. It is also its strength.

Notes

1 See for example Subhash C. Kashyap, *Parliament of India: Myths and Realities,* National Publishing House, New Delhi, 1988, chapter 4. On the other hand an Australian practitioner has expressed the view that the rigidity of party discipline in his country threatens the effectiveness of Parliament to the point where there is a need to re-examine its role in the political process.

Appendix

Appendix

PARLIAMENTS OF INDEPENDENT SOVEREIGN STATES AROUND THE WORLD

- The symbol (F) after the name of a country indicates a federal system of government.
- In the case of bicameral Parliaments and others with more than one chamber, the overall designation is shown underlined, the designations of the individual chambers are listed beneath.
- Unless otherwise indicated it may be assumed that members are directly elected by universal suffrage.

COUNTRY	DESIGNATION OF PARLIAMENT	MEMBERSHIP	DURATION
Afghanistan	National Assembly		
	Council of Representatives	235	5 yrs
	Council of Elders	196	3 yrs to 5 years
		(2 elected from each of the 28 provinces for 5 years, 2 from each Provincial Council elected by the Council for 3 years, remaining appointed by President of the Republic for 3 years)	
Albania	People's Assembly	250	4 yrs
Algeria	National People's Assembly	261	5 yrs
Angola	National People's Assembly	223 (203 elected by electoral colleges, 20 nominated by central committee of the party)	3 yrs
Antigua and Barbuda	Parliament		
	Senate	17 (appointed)	5 yrs
	House of Representatives	17	5 yrs
Argentina (F)	National Congress		
	Senate	46 (nominated by provincial legislatures)	9 yrs (one-third retiring every 3 yrs)
	Chamber of Deputies	254	4 yrs
Australia (F)	Parliament		
	Senate	64	6 yrs (one-half retiring every three years)
	House of Representatives	125	3 yrs
Austria (F)	National Assembly		
	Federal Council (Bundesrat)	63 (elected by the provincial assemblies)	Varying terms
	National Council (Nationalrat)	183	4 yrs
Bahamas	Parliament		
	Senate	16 (appointed)	5 yrs
	House of Assembly	49	5 yrs

143

COUNTRY	DESIGNATION OF PARLIAMENT	MEMBERSHIP	DURATION
Bangladesh	National Assembly	330 (including 30 women appointed by the directly elected members)	5 yrs
Barbados	Parliament Senate	21 (appointed)	5 yrs
	House of Assembly	27	5 yrs
Belgium (F)	Legislative Chambers Senate	182 (106 directly elected)	4 yrs
	Chamber of Representatives	212	4 yrs
Belize	National Assembly Senate	8 (appointed)	5 yrs
	House of Representatives	28	5 yrs
Benin	National Revolutionary Assembly	196	5 yrs
Bhutan	National Assembly (Tshogdu)	151 (106 directly elected)	3 yrs
Bolivia	National Congress Chamber of Senators	27	4 yrs
	Chamber of Deputies	134	4 yrs
Botswana	National Assembly	41 (34 directly elected. Pres. of the Republic is ex-officio member)	5 yrs
Brazil (F)	National Congress Federal Senate	72	8 yrs (Election every 4 yrs renewing alternately 1/3 and 2/3 Senators)
	Chamber of Deputies	487	4 yrs
Bulgaria	National Assembly	400	5 yrs
Burma	People's Assembly	489 (475 directly elected)	4 yrs
Cameroon	National Assembly	180	5 yrs
Canada (F)	Parliament Senate	104 (appointed)	Permanent body (Senators retire at age 75)
	House of Commons	295	5 yrs

COUNTRY	DESIGNATION OF PARLIAMENT	MEMBERSHIP	DURATION
Cape Verde	People's National Assembly	83	5 yrs
Central African Republic	National Assembly	52	5 yrs
China	National People's Congress	2978 (indirectly elected)	5 yrs
Colombia	Congress Senate House of Representatives	112 199	4 yrs 4 yrs
Comoros (F)	Federal Assembly	38	5 yrs
Congo	People's National Assembly	153	5 yrs
Costa Rica	Legislative Assembly	57	4 yrs
Côte d'Ivoire	National Assembly	175	5 yrs
Cuba	National Assembly of People's Power	510 (indirectly elected)	5 yrs
Cyprus	House of Representatives	50	5 yrs
Czechoslovakia (F)	Federal Assembly Chamber of Nations Chamber of the People	150 200	5 yrs 5 yrs
Denmark	Folketing	179	4 yrs
Djibouti	Chamber of Deputies	65	5 yrs
Dominica	House of Assembly	30 (21 directly elected)	5 yrs
Dominican Republic	Congress Senate Chamber of Deputies	30 120	4 yrs 4 yrs
Ecuador	National Congress	71	2 yrs (12 members elected on a national basis serve a 4 yr term)
Egypt	People's Assembly (Majlis Ash-Sha'ab)	458 (448 directly elected)	5 yrs

145

COUNTRY	DESIGNATION OF PARLIAMENT	MEMBERSHIP	DURATION
El Salvador	Legislative Assembly	60	3 yrs
Equatorial Guinea	House of Representatives of the People	60	5 yrs
Ethiopia	National Assembly (Shengo)	813	5 yrs
Finland	Eduskunta	200	4 yrs
France	Parliament Senate National Assembly	319 (indirectly elected) 577	9 yrs (one-third retiring every three years) 5 yrs
Gabon	National Assembly	120 (111 directly elected)	5 yrs
Gambia	House of Representatives	50 (36 directly elected)	5 yrs
German Democratic Republic	People's Chamber (Volkskammer)	500	5 yrs
Germany (Federal Republic of) (F)	Parliament Federal Council (Bundesrat) Federal Assembly (Bundestag)	45 (appointed by the state governments) 519 (including 22 members from West Berlin with limited voting rights)	Appointments made or renewed after each state election 4 yrs
Greece	Chamber of Deputies	300 (maximum)	4 yrs
Grenada	Parliament Senate House of Representatives	13 (appointed) 15	5 yrs 5 yrs
Guatemala	Congress	100	5 yrs
Guinea-Bissau	National People's Assembly	150 (indirectly elected)	5 yrs
Guyana	National Assembly	65 (53 directly elected)	5 yrs
Honduras	National Congress	134	4 yrs

146

COUNTRY	DESIGNATION OF PARLIAMENT	MEMBERSHIP	DURATION
Hungary	National Assembly	387 (includes 35 eminent persons elected at large)	5 yrs
Iceland	Althing		
	Eefri Deild	21 (Members separate into two Houses following each general election)	4 yrs
	Nedri Deild	42	4 yrs
India (F)	Parliament		
	Council of States (Rajya Sabha)	250 (maximum. The majority indirectly elected by the state assemblies, the remainder appointed.)	6 yrs (one-third retiring every 2 yrs)
	House of the People (Lok Sabha)	544 (542 directly elected)	5 yrs
Indonesia	People's Consultative Assembly	1000	5 yrs
	House of Representatives	500 (400 directly elected. Remaining seats allocated to regions, Armed Forces and other organisations, in proportion to their elected seats)	5 yrs
Iran (Islamic Republic of)	Islamic Consultative Assembly (Majlis)	270	4 yrs
Iraq	National Assembly	250	4 yrs
Ireland	Parliament (Oireachtas)		
	Senate (Seanad Eireann)	60 (some indirectly elected, some nominated)	5 yrs
	House of Representatives (Dail Eireann)	166	5 yrs
Israel	Knesset	120	4 yrs
Italy	Parliament		
	Senate	323	5 yrs
	Chamber of Deputies	630	5 yrs
Jamaica	Parliament		
	Senate	21 (appointed)	5 yrs
	House of Representatives	60	5 yrs
Japan	Diet		
	House of Councillors	252 (one-half elected every 3 years)	6 yrs
	House of Representatives	512	4 yrs

147

COUNTRY	DESIGNATION OF PARLIAMENT	MEMBERSHIP	DURATION
Jordan	National Assembly		
	Senate	30 (appointed)	4 yrs
	House of Deputies	60	4 yrs
Kenya	National Assembly	188 (12 additional members are nominated by the President)	5 yrs
Kiribati	House of Assembly	39 (36 directly elected)	4 yrs
Korea (Democratic People's Republic of)	Supreme People's Assembly	655	4 yrs
Korea (Republic of)	National Assembly	276	4 yrs
Lebanon	National Assembly	99	4 yrs (No election has taken place since 1972 and the term of the Assembly is currently extended to 1990)
Liberia	National Assembly		
	Senate	26	6 yrs
	House of Representatives	64	4 yrs
Liechtenstein	Landtag	25	4 yrs
Luxembourg	Chamber of Deputies	64	5 yrs
Madagascar	National People's Assembly	137	5 yrs
Malawi	National Assembly	112 (An unlimited number of additional members may be appointed by the President	5 yrs
Malaysia (F)	Parliament		
	Senate (Dewan Negara)	68 (42 appointed, 26 elected by state legislatures)	3 yrs
	House of Representatives (Dewan Rakyat)	177	5 yrs
Maldives	Citizen's Majlis	48 (40 directly elected)	5 yrs

PARLIAMENTS OF INDEPENDENT SOVEREIGN STATES AROUND THE WORLD

COUNTRY	DESIGNATION OF PARLIAMENT	MEMBERSHIP	DURATION
Mali	National Assembly	82	3 yrs
Malta	House of Representatives	69	5 yrs
Mauritius	Legislative Assembly	70 (62 directly elected)	5 yrs
Mexico (F)	General Congress Senate	64	6 yrs (half retiring every three years)
	Chamber of Deputies	400	3 yrs
Monaco	National Council	18	5 yrs
Mongolia	Great People's Khural	370	5 yrs
Morocco	House of Representatives	306 (206 directly elected)	6 yrs
Mozambique	People's Assembly	250 (indirectly elected)	5 yrs
Nauru	Parliament	18	3 yrs
Nepal	National Assembly (Rashtriya Panchayat)	140 (112 directly elected)	5 yrs
Netherlands	States General First Chamber	75 (elected by the provincial councils)	4 yrs
	Second Chamber	150	4 yrs
New Zealand	House of Representatives	97 (4 seats reserved for Maoris)	3 yrs
Nicaragua	National Assembly	96 (90 directly elected)	6 yrs
Norway	Storting Lagting	39 (Members separate into two Houses following each general election)	4 yrs
	Odelsting	118	4 yrs
Pakistan (F)	Parliament (Majlis-E-Shoora) Senate	87 (76 elected by provincial assemblies, 11 by other means)	6 yrs
	National Assembly (please see overleaf)		

COUNTRY	DESIGNATION OF PARLIAMENT	MEMBERSHIP	DURATION
Pakistan (cont.)	National Assembly	237 (217 directly elected, 20 seats reserved for women elected by provincial assemblies)	5 yrs
Panama	Legislative Assembly	67	5 yrs
Papua New Guinea	National Parliament	109	5 yrs
Paraguay	Congress Senate Chamber of Deputies	 30 60	 5 yrs 5 yrs
Peru	Congress Senate Chamber of Deputies	 60 180	 5 yrs 5 yrs
Philippines	Congress Senate House of Representatives	 24 250 (maximum: 200 directly elected)	 6 yrs 3 yrs
Poland	National Assembly Senate Sejm	 100 460 (includes 35 eminent persons elected for special seats)	 4 yrs 4 yrs
Portugal	Assembly of the Republic	250	4 yrs
Romania	Grand National Assembly	369	5 yrs
Rwanda	National Development Council	70	5 yrs
St. Christopher-Nevis (St. Kitts-Nevis)	National Assembly (Nevis also has its own Island Assembly, partly elected, partly nominated)	16 (11 directly elected)	5 yrs
St. Lucia	Parliament Senate House of Assembly	 11 (appointed) 17	 5 yrs 5 yrs
St. Vincent and the Grenadines	House of Assembly	19 (13 directly elected)	5 yrs
Samoa (Western)	Legislative Assembly	47 (45 elected by local custom from the matais, 2 by universal suffrage)	3 yrs

150

PARLIAMENTS OF INDEPENDENT SOVEREIGN STATES AROUND THE WORLD

COUNTRY	DESIGNATION OF PARLIAMENT	MEMBERSHIP	DURATION
San Marino	Great and General Council	60	5 yrs
Sao Tomé e Principe	National People's Assembly	40	5 yrs
Senegal	National Assembly	120	5 yrs
Seychelles	People's Assembly	25 (23 directly elected)	5 yrs
Sierra Leone	Parliament	124 (105 directly elected)	5 yrs
Singapore	Parliament	81	5 yrs
Solomon Islands	National Parliament	38	4 yrs
Somalia	People's Assembly	177 (171 directly elected)	5 yrs
South Africa	Parliament House of Assembly (consisting of white members)	178 (166 directly elected by white electorate)	5 yrs
	House of Representatives (consisting of Coloured members)	85 (80 directly elected by Coloured electorate)	5 yrs
	House of Delegates (consisting of Indian members)	45 (40 directly elected by Indian electorate)	5 yrs
Spain	Cortes Senate	257 (208 directly elected)	4 yrs
	Congress of Deputies	350	4 yrs
Sri Lanka	Parliament	168	6 yrs
Sudan	Constituent Assembly (Constitution suspended June 1989)	301 (including 28 members elected by graduates of universities and polytechnics)	4 yrs
Suriname	National Assembly	51	5 yrs
Swaziland	Parliament Senate	20 (10 indirectly elected, 10 appointed)	5 yrs
	House of Assembly	50 (40 indirectly elected, 10 appointed)	5 yrs

151

COUNTRY	DESIGNATION OF PARLIAMENT	MEMBERSHIP	DURATION
Sweden	Riksdag	349	3 yrs
Switzerland (F)	Federal Assembly Council of States (Ständerat) National Council (Nationalrat)	46 (method of election determined by the cantons) 200	Tenure of office determined by the cantons. 4 yrs
Syrian Arab Republic	People's Council	195	4 yrs
Tanzania (United Republic of)	National Assembly	244 (169 directly elected)	5 yrs
Thailand	National Assembly Senate House of Representatives	268 (appointed) 347	6 yrs 4 yrs
Togo	National Assembly	77	5 yrs
Tonga	Legislative Assembly	29 (9 directly elected)	3 yrs
Trinidad and Tobago	Parliament Senate House of Representatives (Note: Tobago also has its own House of Assembly of 15 members, 12 of whom are directly elected)	31 (appointed) 36	5 yrs 5 yrs
Tunisia	National Assembly	125	5 yrs
Turkey	Grand National Assembly	460	5 yrs
Tuvalu	Parliament	12	4 yrs
Union of Soviet Socialist Republics (F)	Congress of People's Deputies (highest body of state authority, elected by various methods) Supreme Soviet Soviet of Nationalities Soviet of the Union	2250 271 271	The Supreme Soviet is elected by the Congress of People's Deputies from their own number, one-fifth being re-elected annually
United Arab Emirates (F)	Federal National Council	40 (appointed)	2 yrs

PARLIAMENTS OF INDEPENDENT SOVEREIGN STATES AROUND THE WORLD

COUNTRY	DESIGNATION OF PARLIAMENT	MEMBERSHIP	DURATION
United Kingdom	Parliament House of Lords	No fixed number. (Currently about 1200, some hereditary, some appointed for life. Also includes 2 archbishops and 24 bishops.)	Permanent body
	House of Commons	650	5 yrs
United States of America (F)	Congress Senate	100	6 yrs (one-third retiring every two years)
	House of Representatives	435	2 yrs
Uruguay	General Assembly Senate	31	5 yrs
	Chamber of Representatives	99	5 yrs
Vanuatu	Parliament	39	4 yrs
Venezuela (F)	Congress Senate	44 (former Presidents of the Republic are also ex-officio members)	5 yrs
	Chamber of Deputies	199	5 yrs
Vietnam	National Assembly	496	5 yrs
Yemen	There are two representative bodies General People's Congress	1000 (700 elected)	4 yrs
	People's Constituent Assembly	159 (128 elected and 31 appointed)	4 yrs
Yemen (Democratic)	Supreme People's Council	111	5 yrs
Yugoslavia (F)	Assembly of the Socialist Federal Republic of Yugoslavia Federal Chamber	220 (indirectly elected)	4 yrs
	Chamber of Republics and Autonomous Provinces	88 (indirectly elected)	4 yrs
Zaire	National Legislative Council	210 (310 prior to 1987)	5 yrs
Zambia	National Assembly	135 (125 directly elected)	5 yrs

COUNTRY	DESIGNATION OF PARLIAMENT	MEMBERSHIP	DURATION
Zimbabwe	Parliament		
	Senate	40 (indirectly elected and partly nominated)	5 yrs
	House of Assembly	100 (80 directly elected, 20 indirectly elected)	5 yrs

154

Index

155

160

163

Information services, 132
International affairs, 46
Laws, constitutionality, 41
Legislative process, 65–7, 70–1
Limiting debate, 93–4
Media, 130
Presiding officer, 52–3, 57–8
Procedure, 62–3
Staff and services, 123–5
State legislatures, 10
Voting methods, 94
Uruguay
Electoral system, 19

Vanuatu
Parliament
Head of state, 38
Languages, 65
Presiding officer, 58–9
Venezuela
Electoral system, 18
Parliament, presiding officer, 59
Voters, 14–5
Qualifications, 14
Age, 14–5
Race, 14
Women, 14
Voting methods see Parliament

West Germany
Electoral system, 17–8
Parliament
Broadcasting, 134
Committees, 104
Composition, 7
Confidence, 87
Government structure,
relationship, 32
Head of state, 38
Immunities, 117, 122
Impeachment, 44
Information services, 131
Interpellation, 88
Laws, constitutionality, 42
Legislative process, 66, 68, 72
Limiting debate, 94
Presiding officer, 55, 58

Staff and services, 125–6
Western Samoa
Parliament, head of state, 37
Women see Electoral systems;
Presiding officers; Voters—
Qualifications

Yugoslavia
Electoral system, 24–5
Parliament
Composition, 2, 8
Confidence, 88
Head of state, 38
Languages, 64
Laws, constitutionality, 42
Legislative process, 66–8
Media, 130
Presiding officer, 56–7
Voting methods, 94

Zaire
One–party system, role, 35
Zambia
One–party system, role, 35
Electoral system, 25, 28
Parliament
Committees, 101
Government structure,
relationship, 31
Cabinet ministers, 31
Head of state, 38
Immunities, 120
Media, 130
Presiding officer, 51
Staff and services, 124
Zimbabwe
Electoral system, 26
Parliament
Composition, 2
Executive, 85
Government structure,
relationship, 35
Head of state, 38
Immunities, 119
Information services, 132
Languages, 65
Presiding officer, 51
Staff and services, 124